For my children Alex and Jack,

without whom I would not be

typing this at 1 a.m.

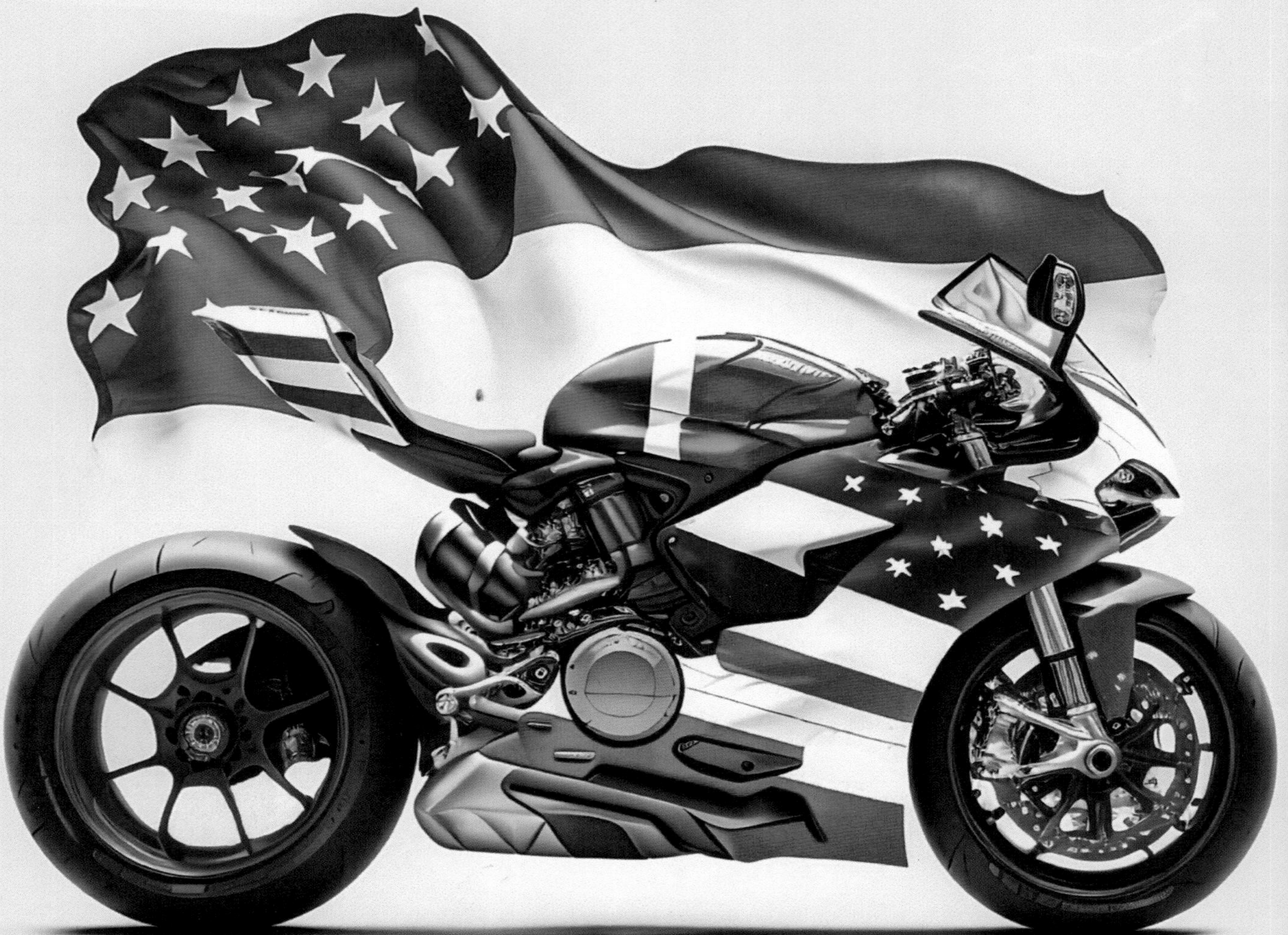

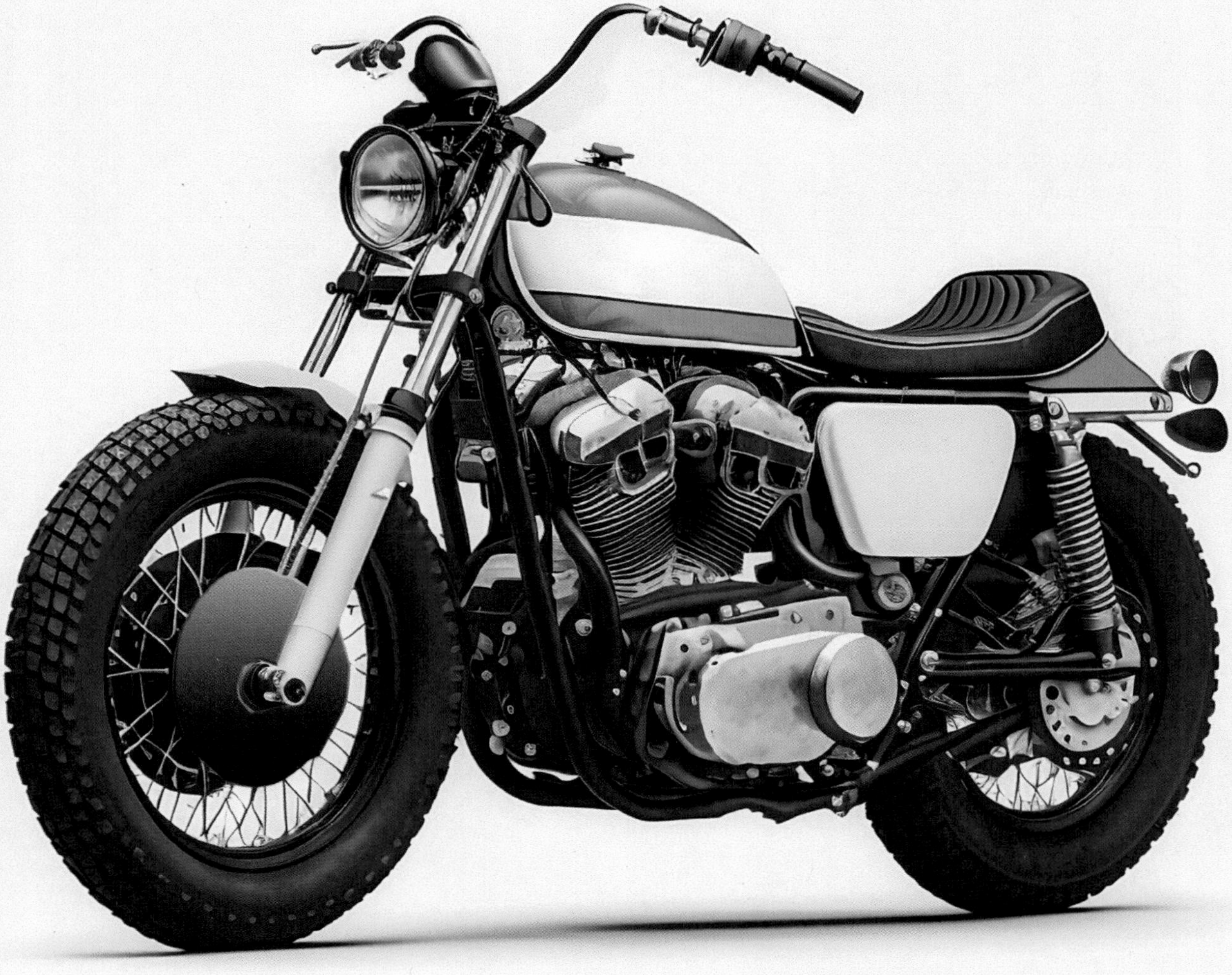

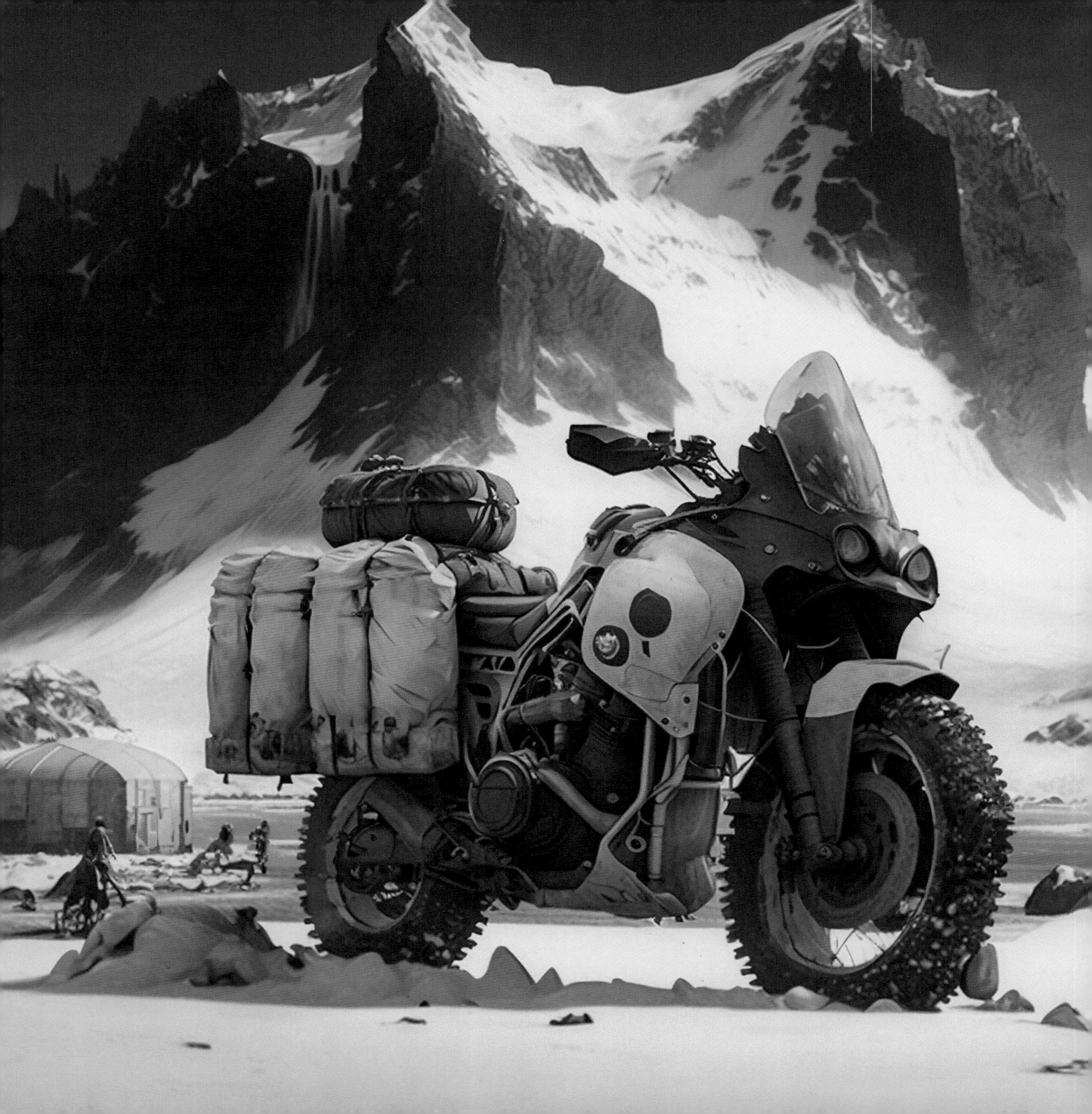

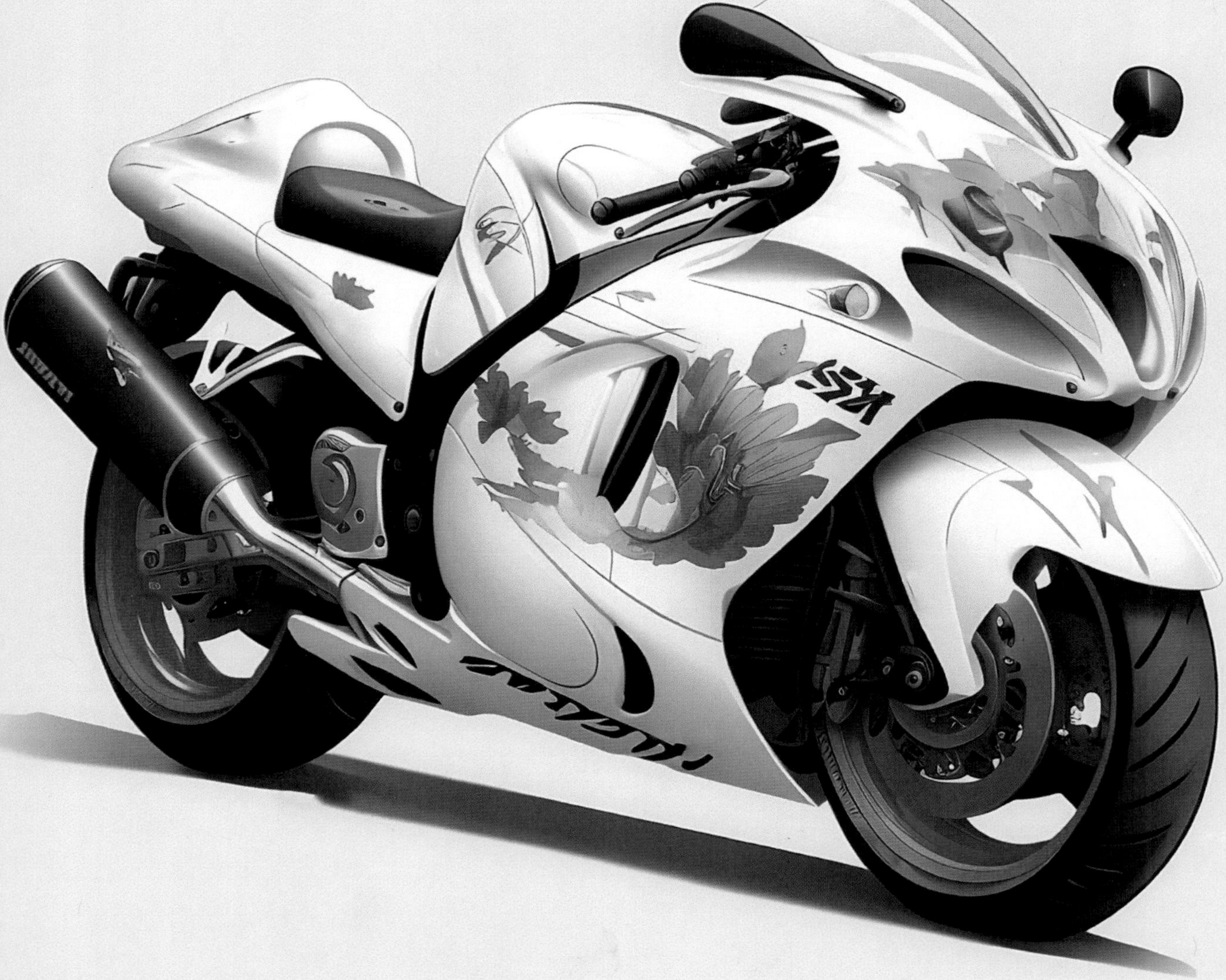

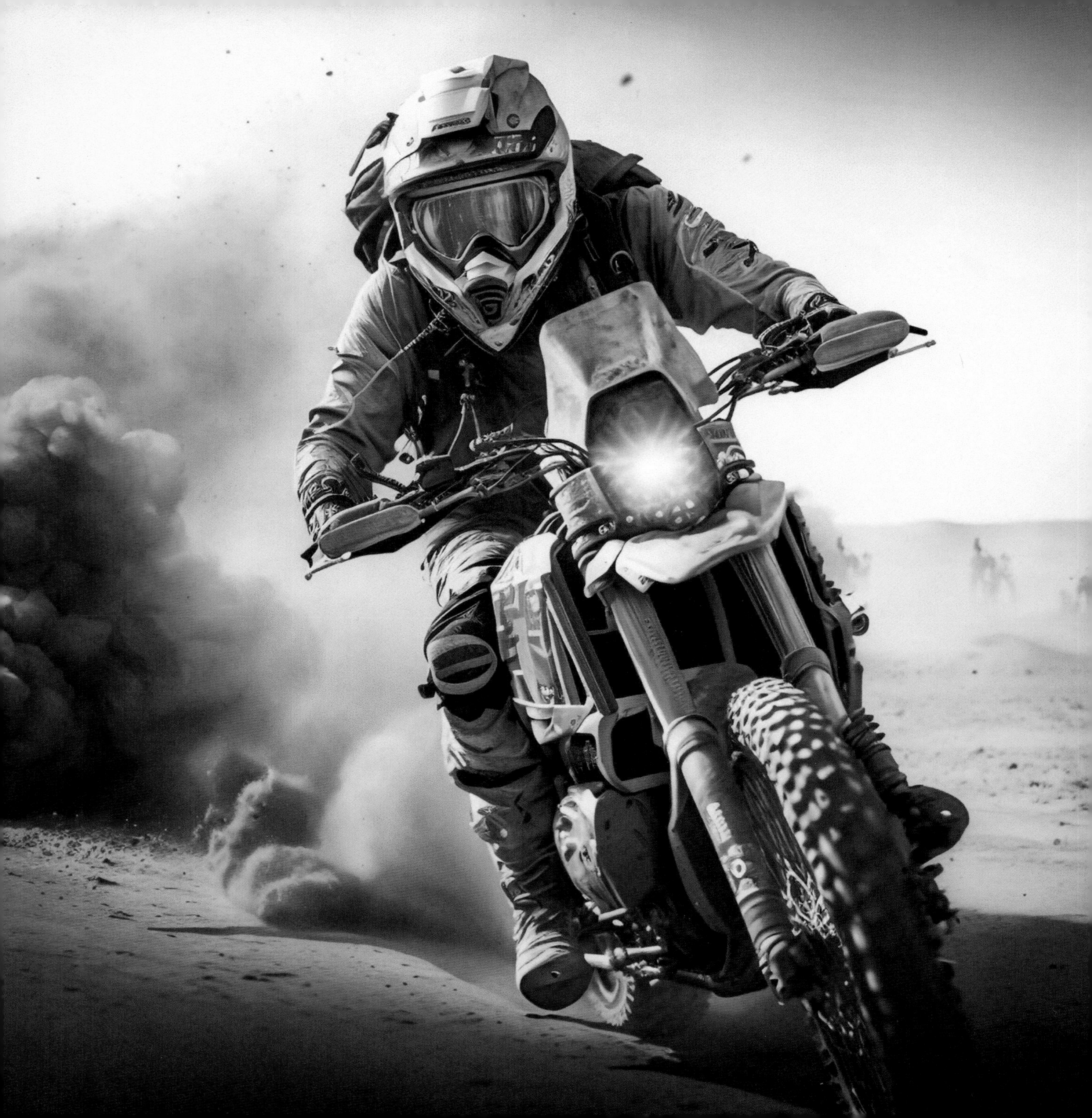

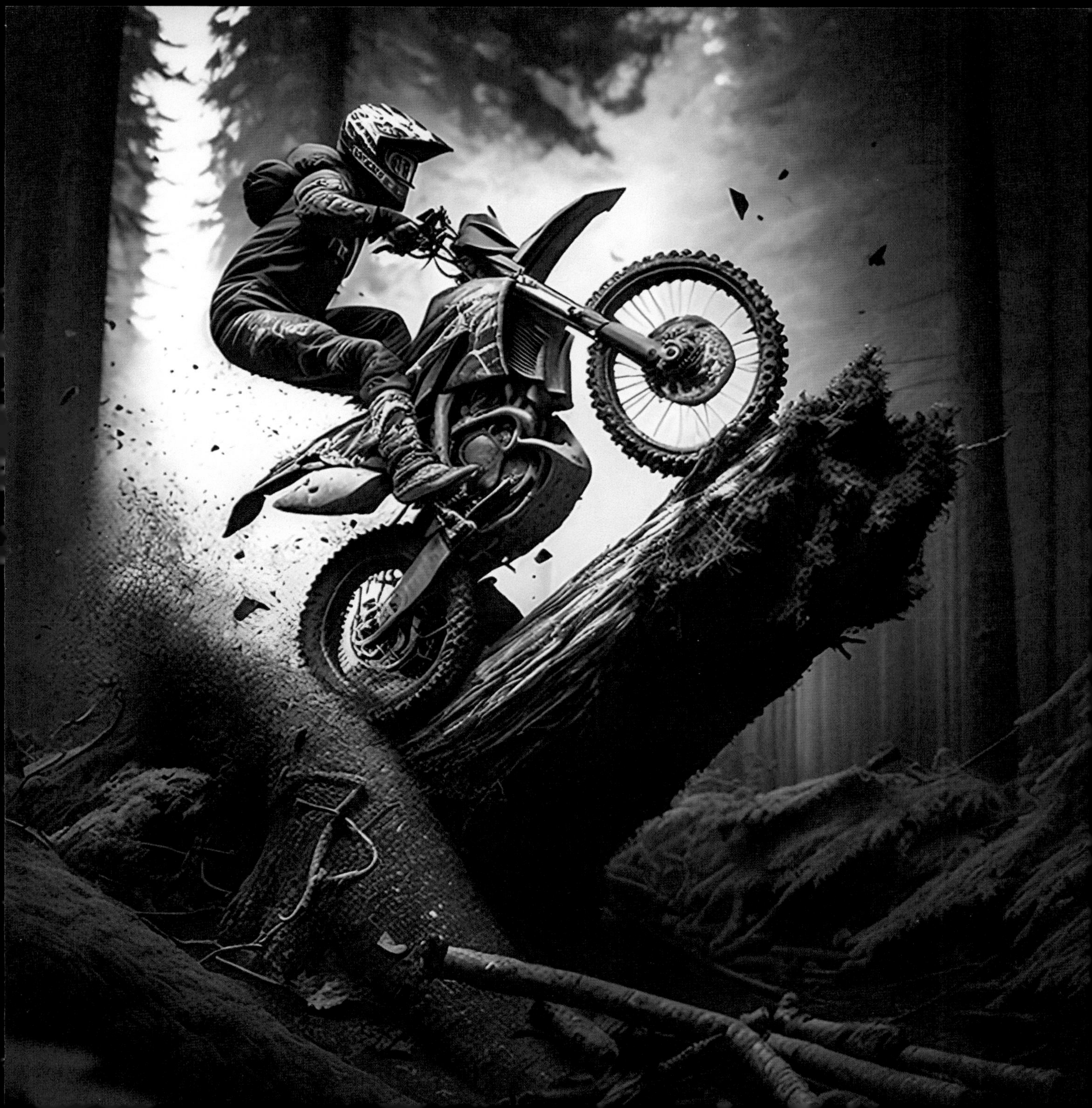

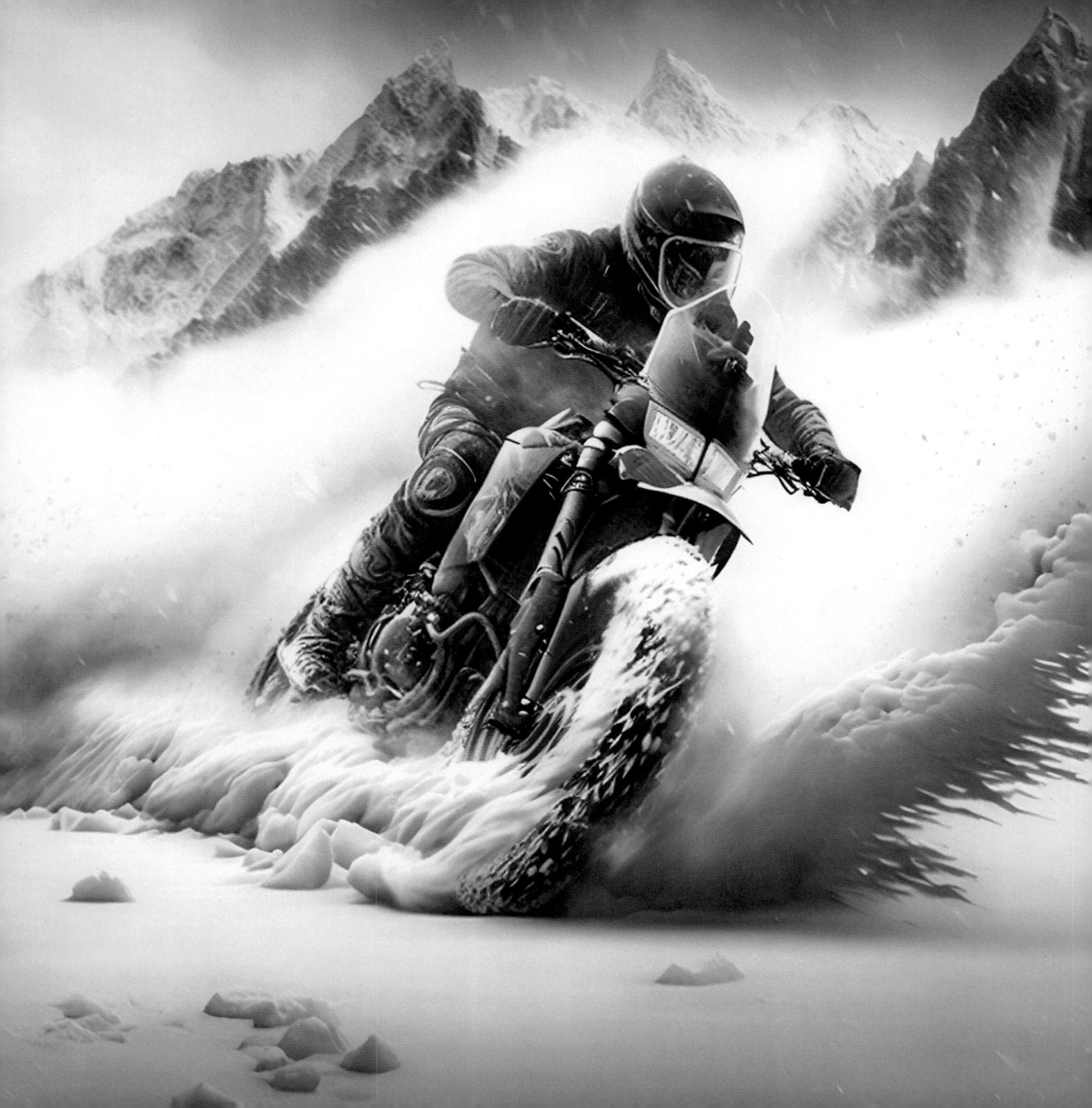

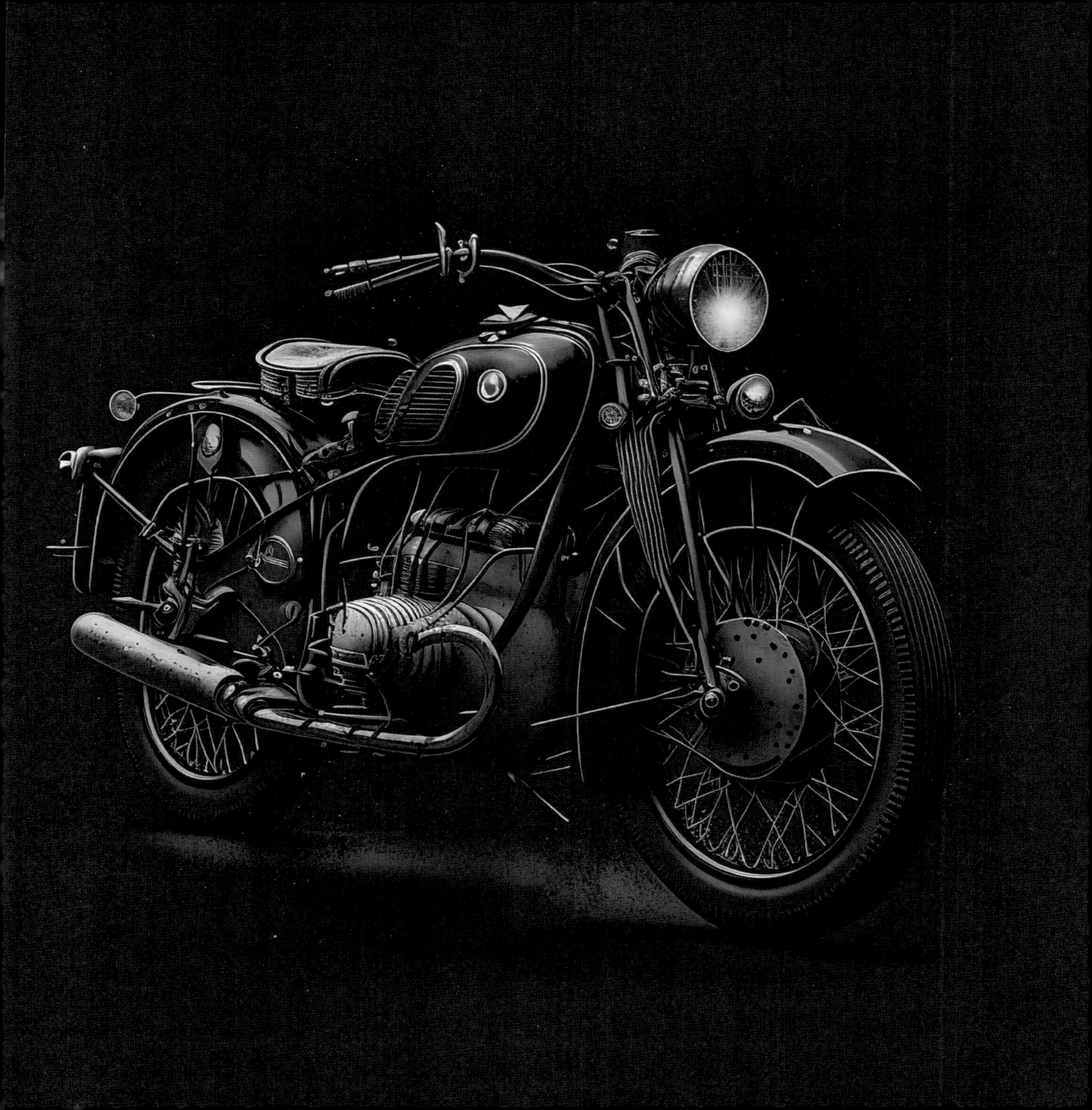

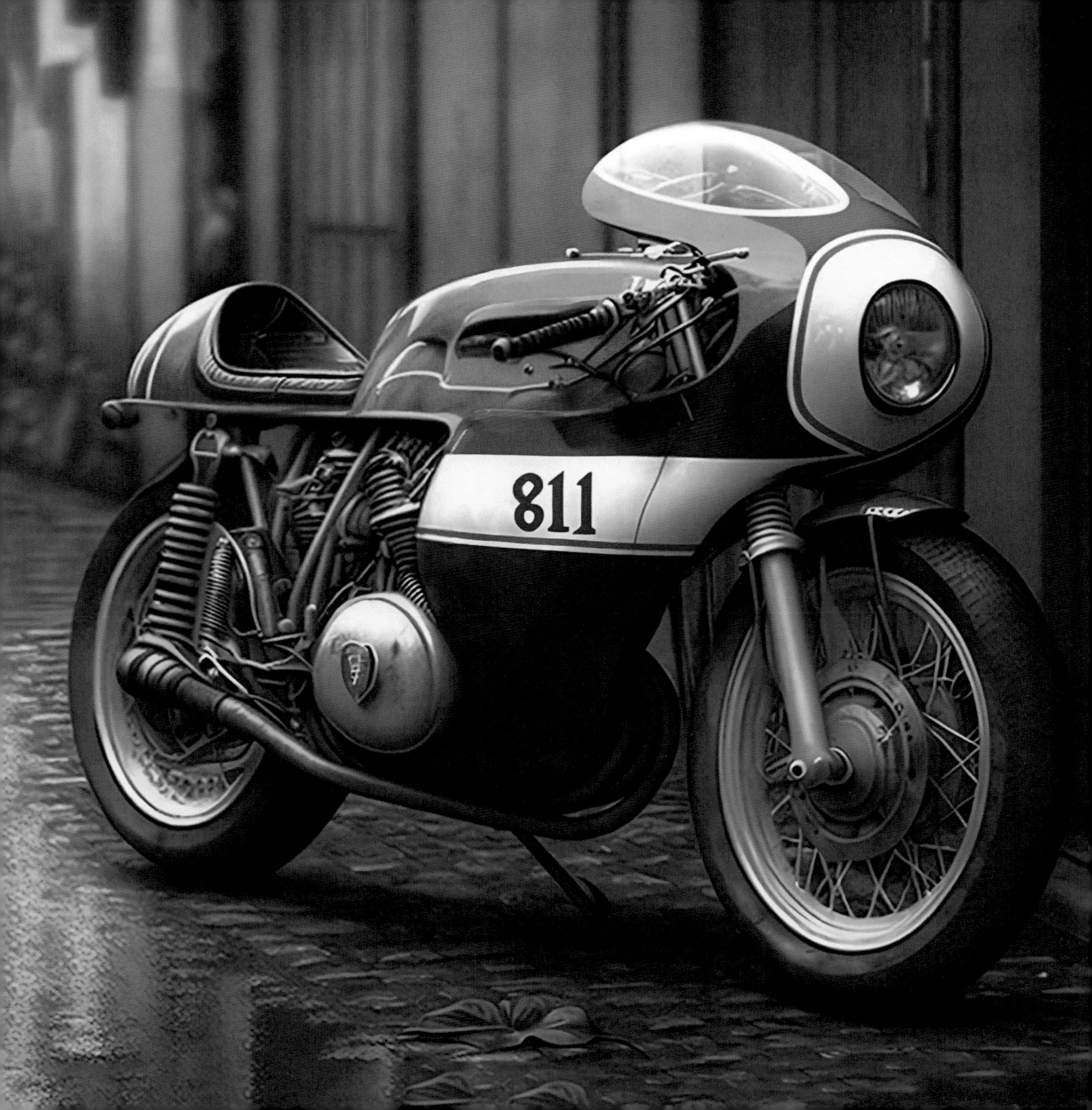
811

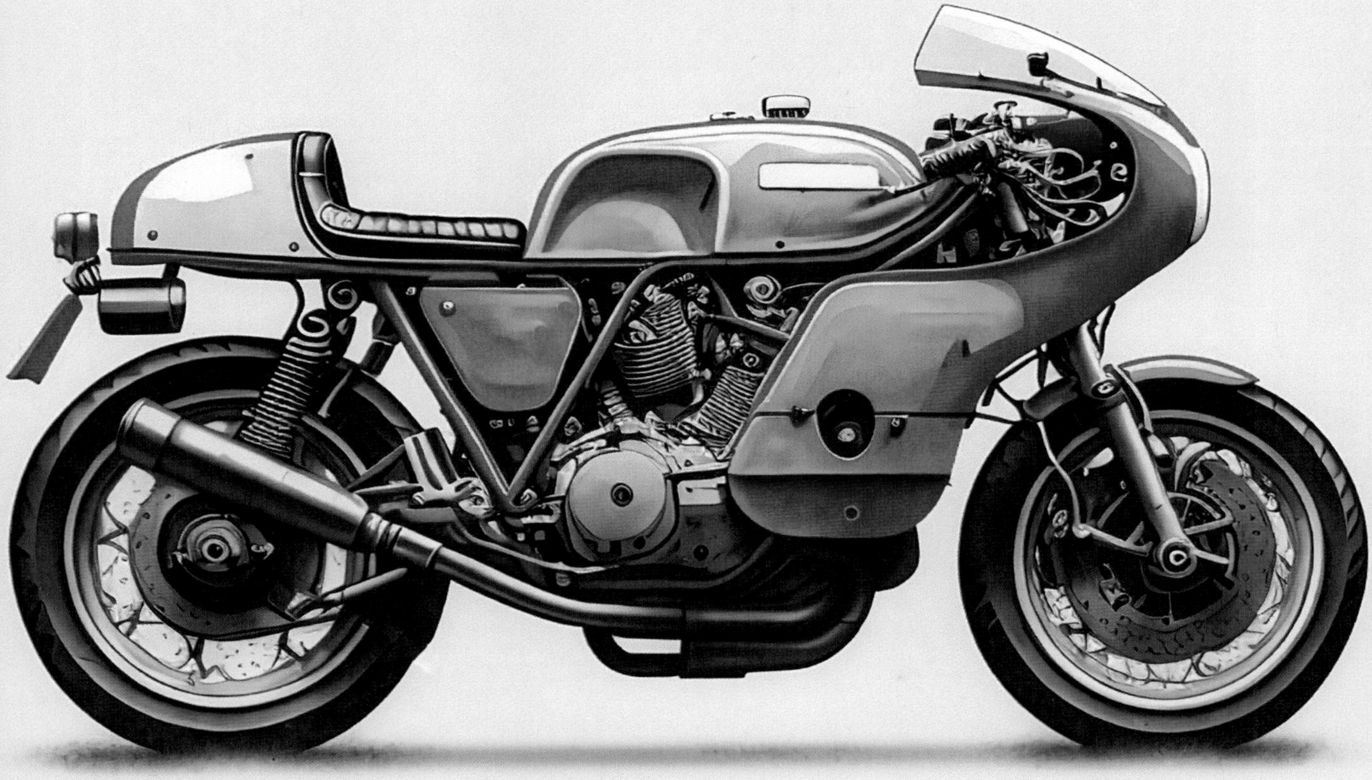

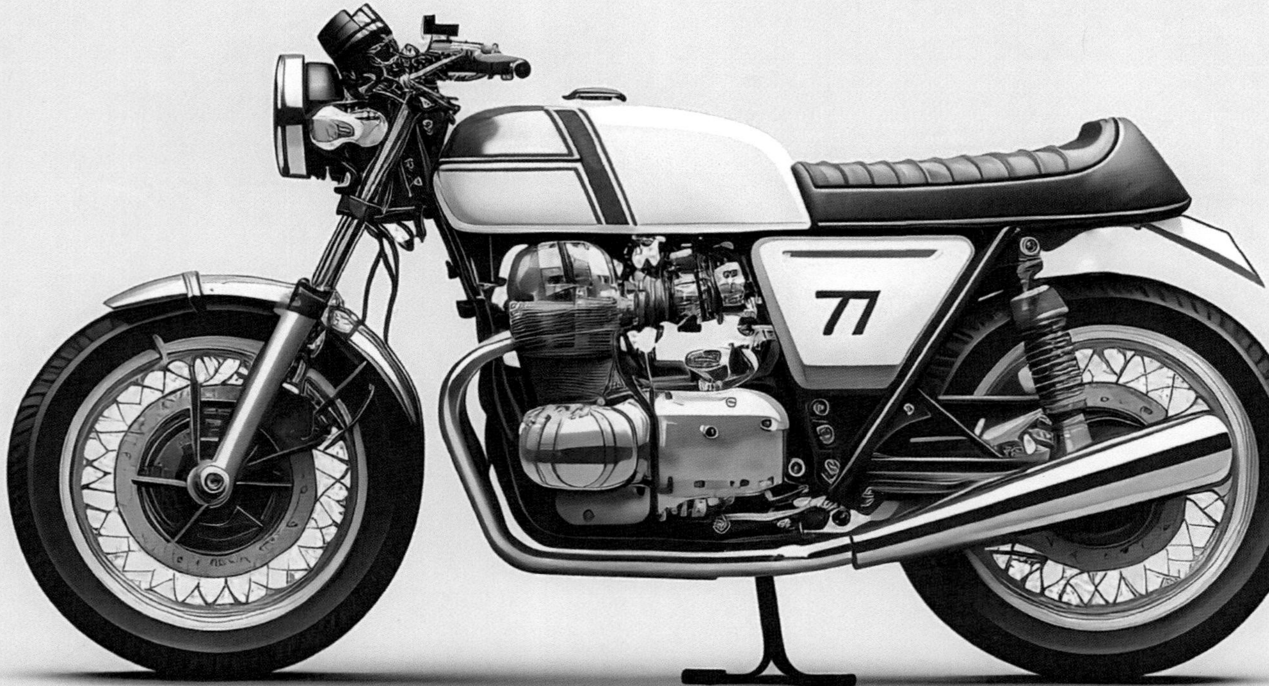
77

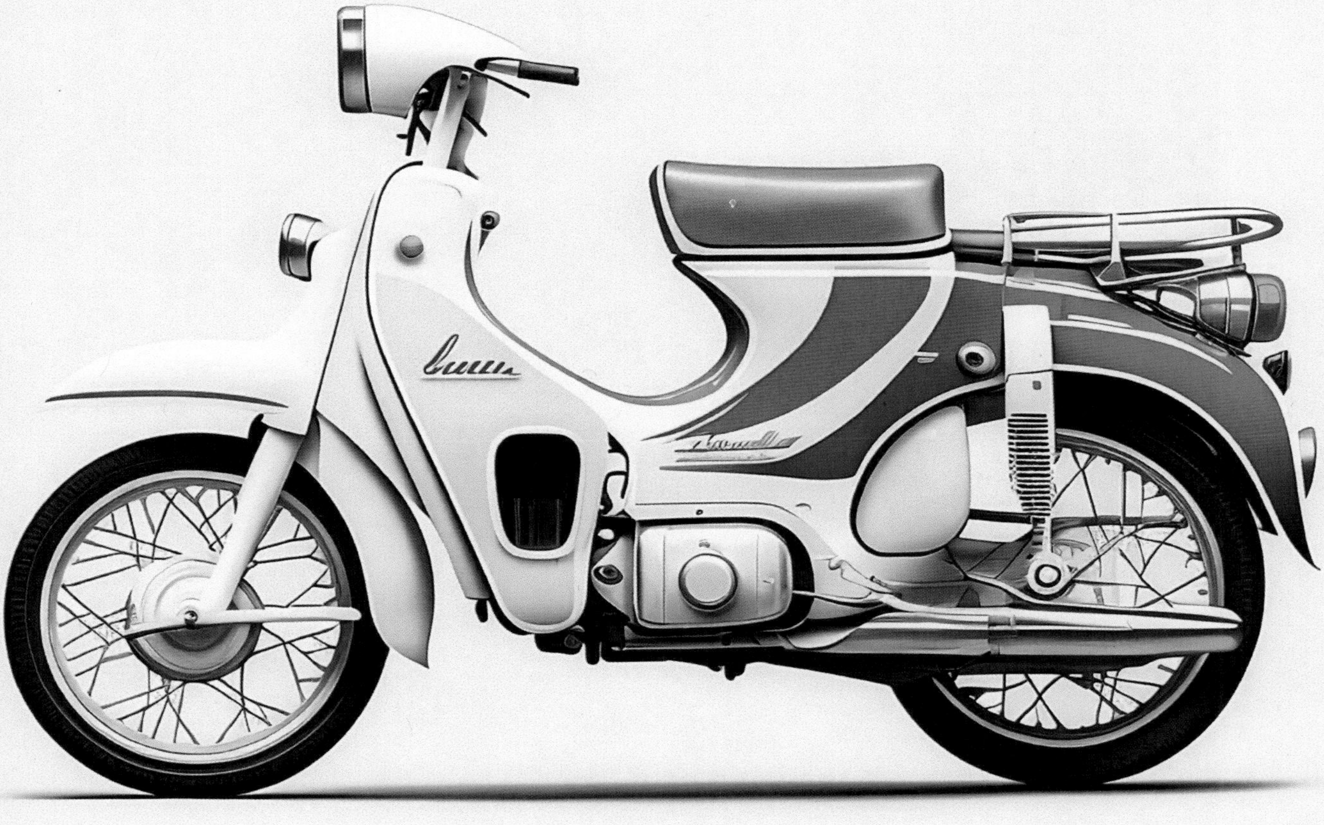

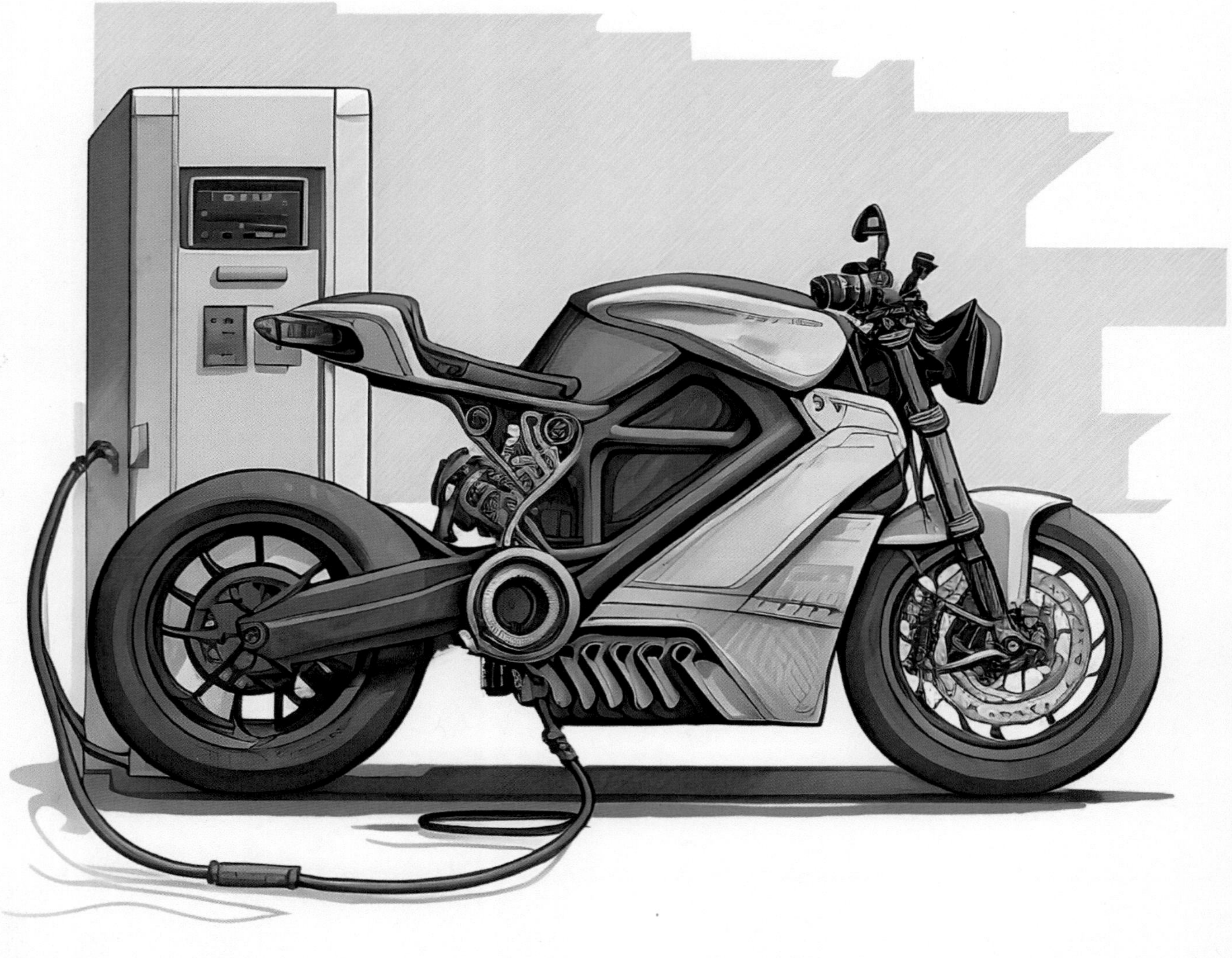

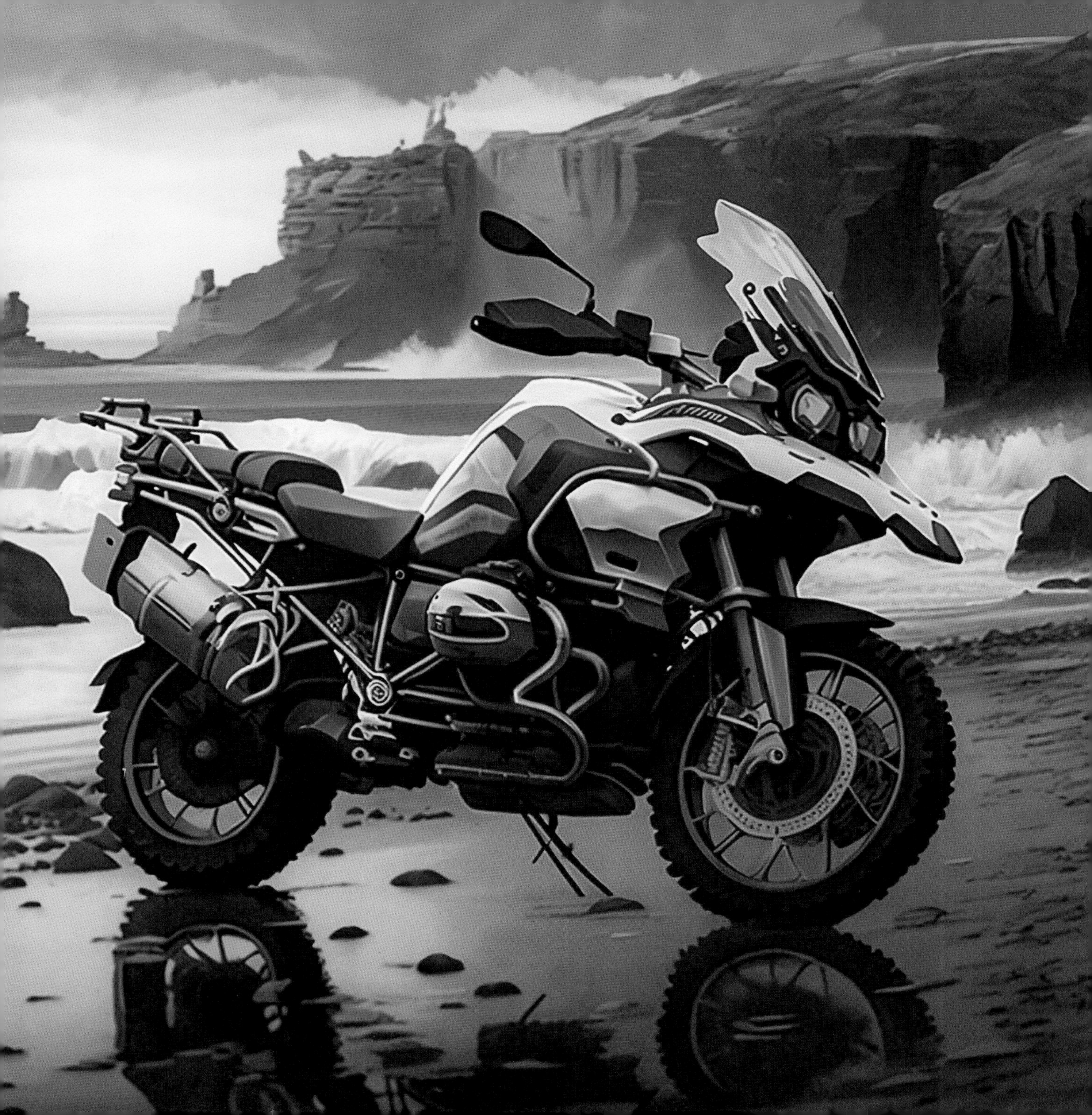

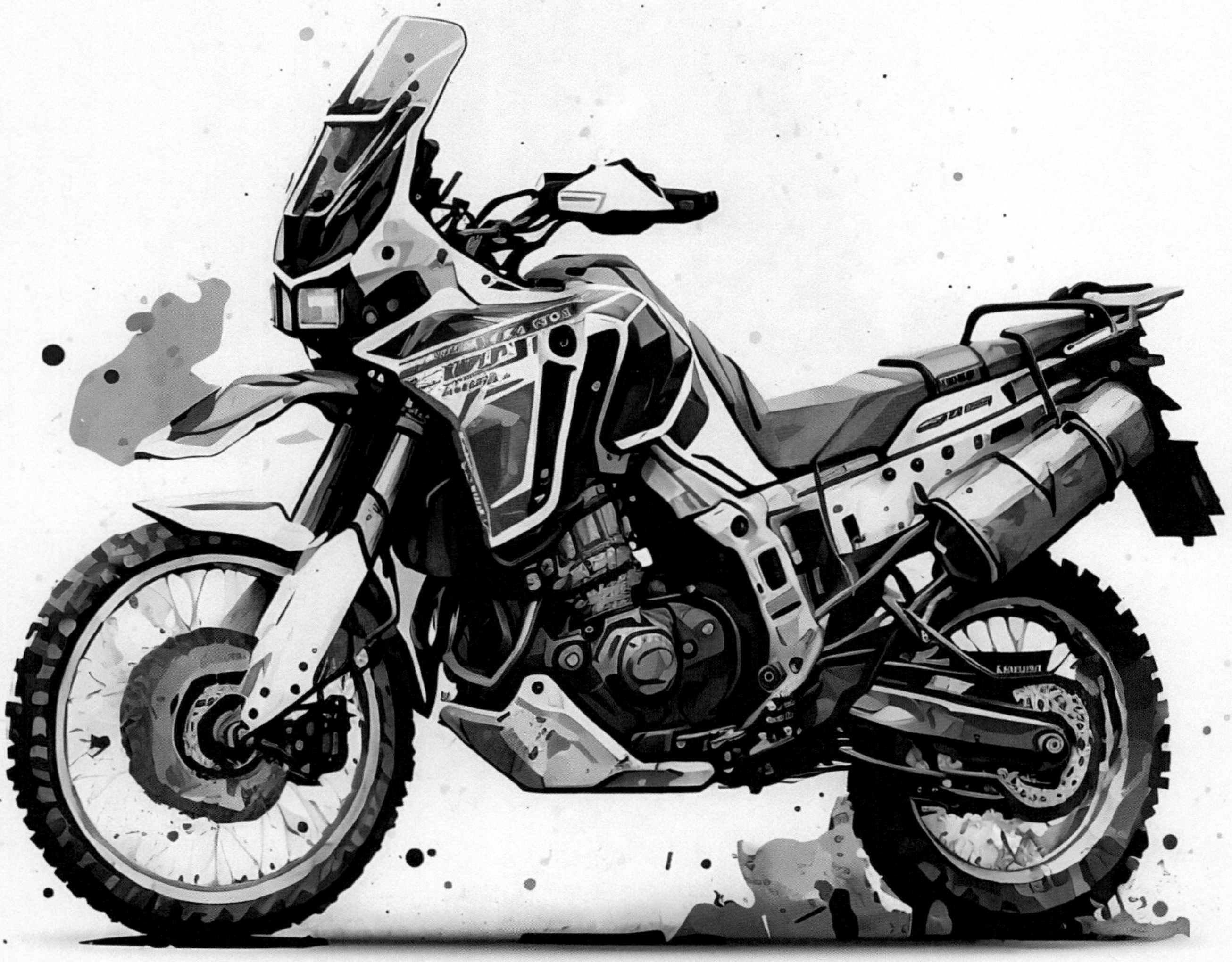

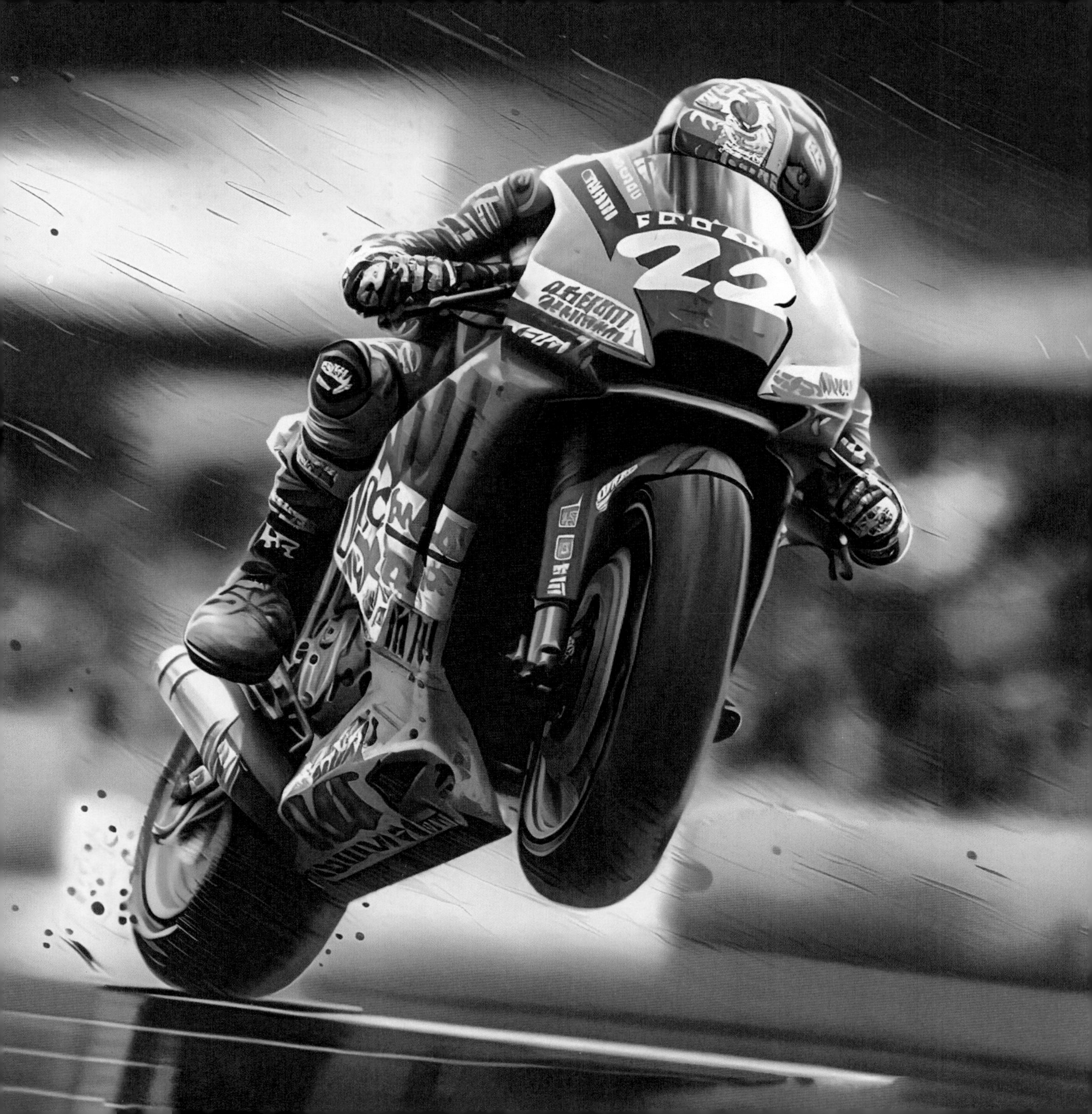
22

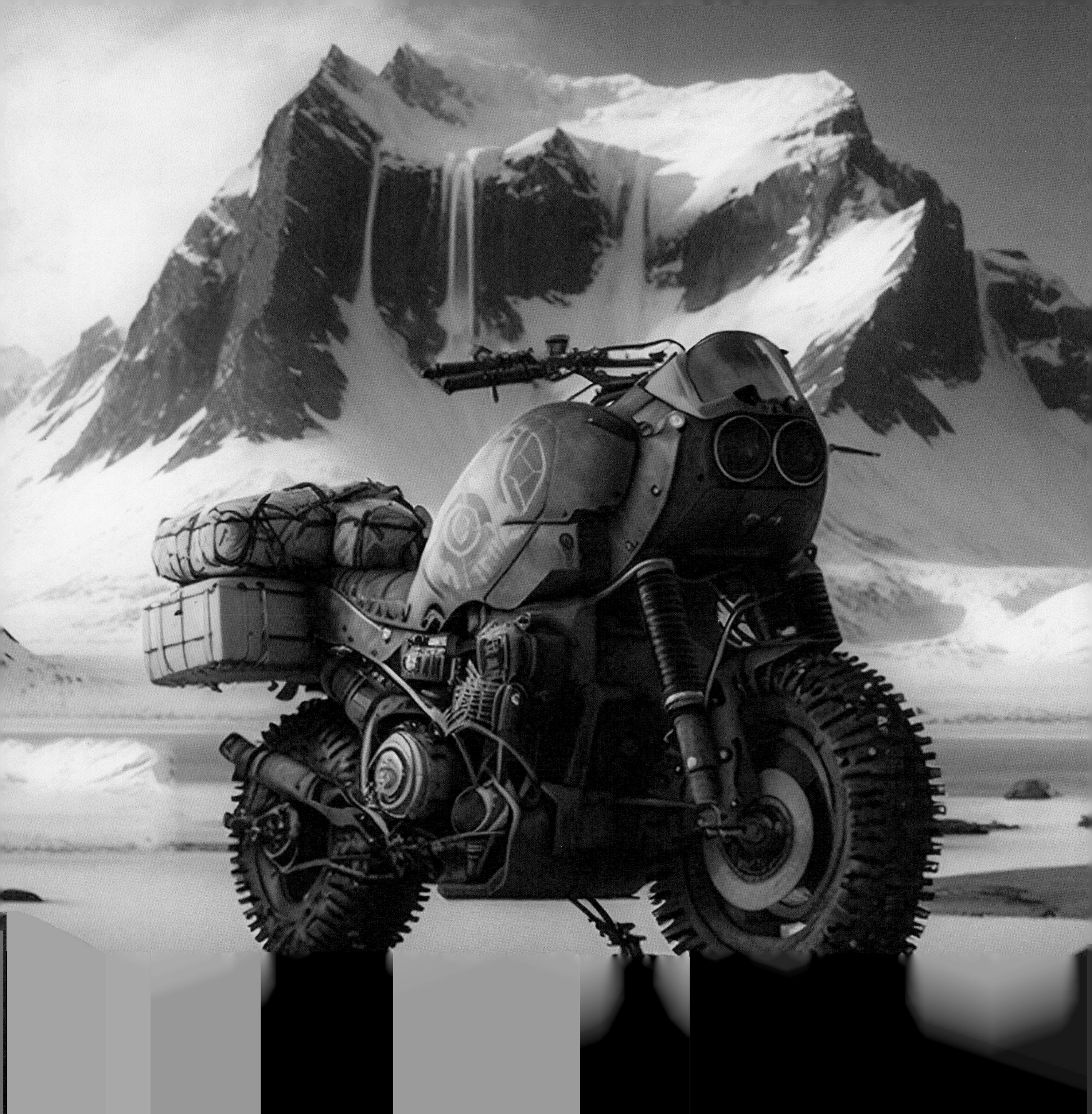

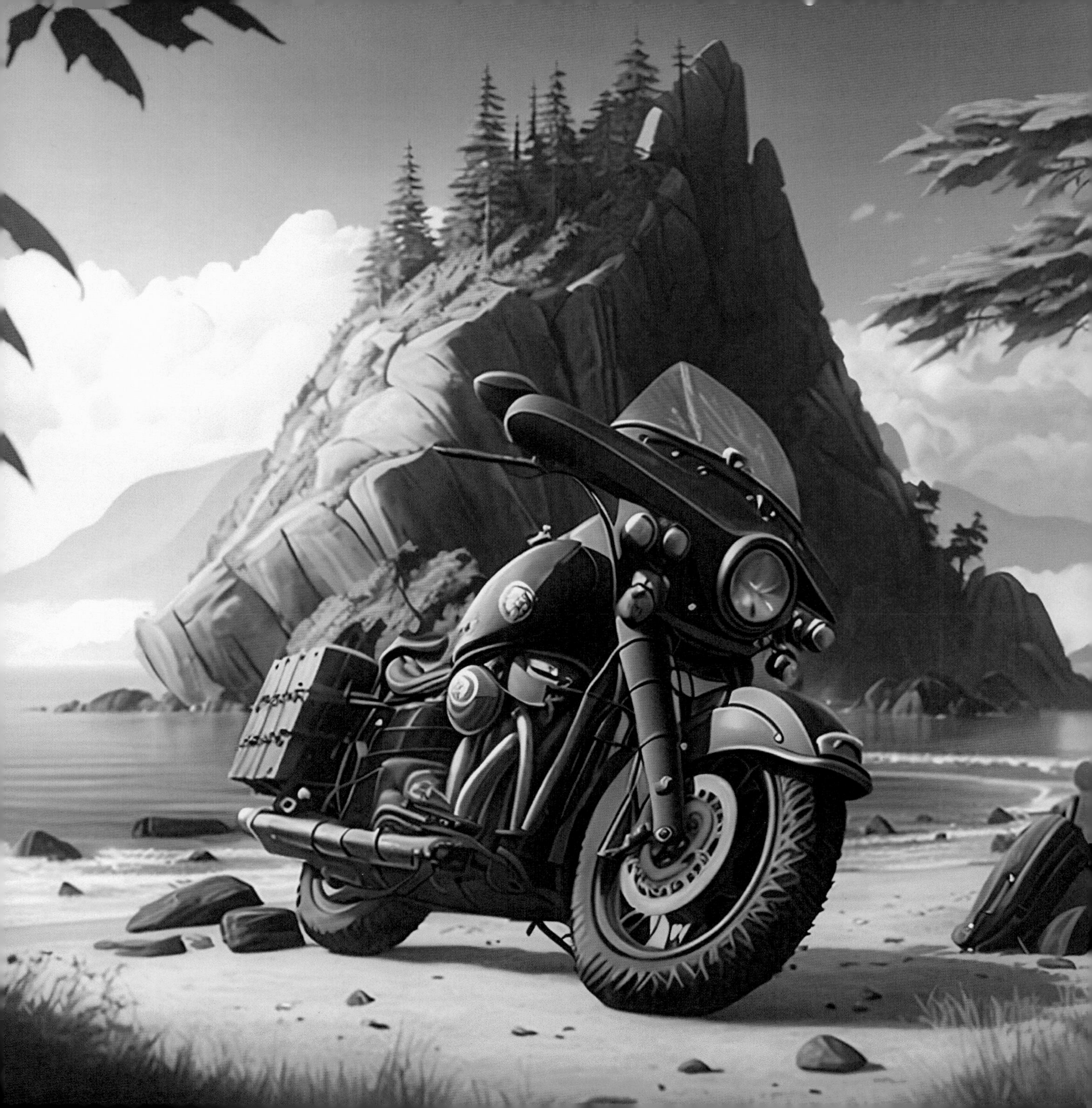

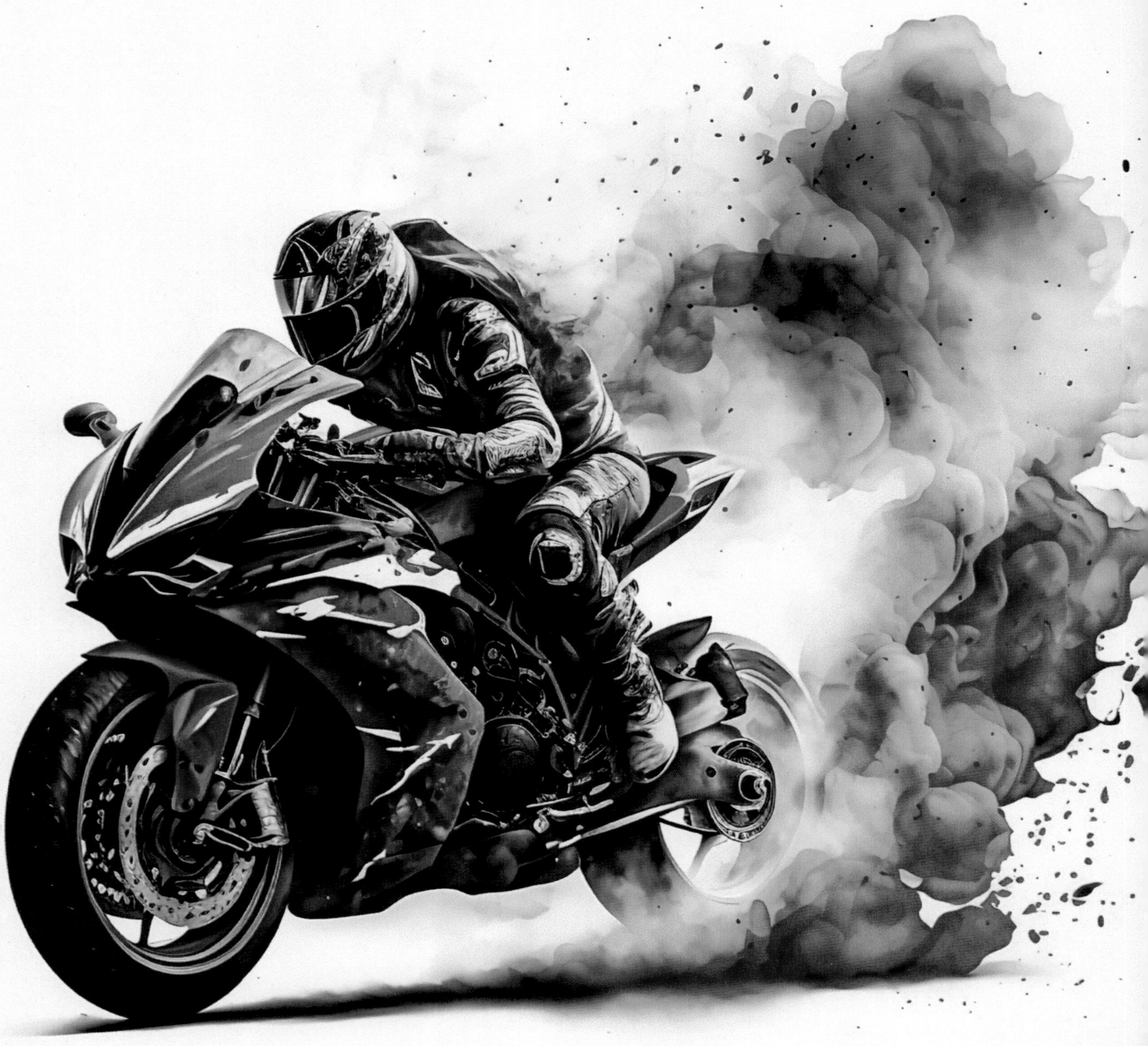

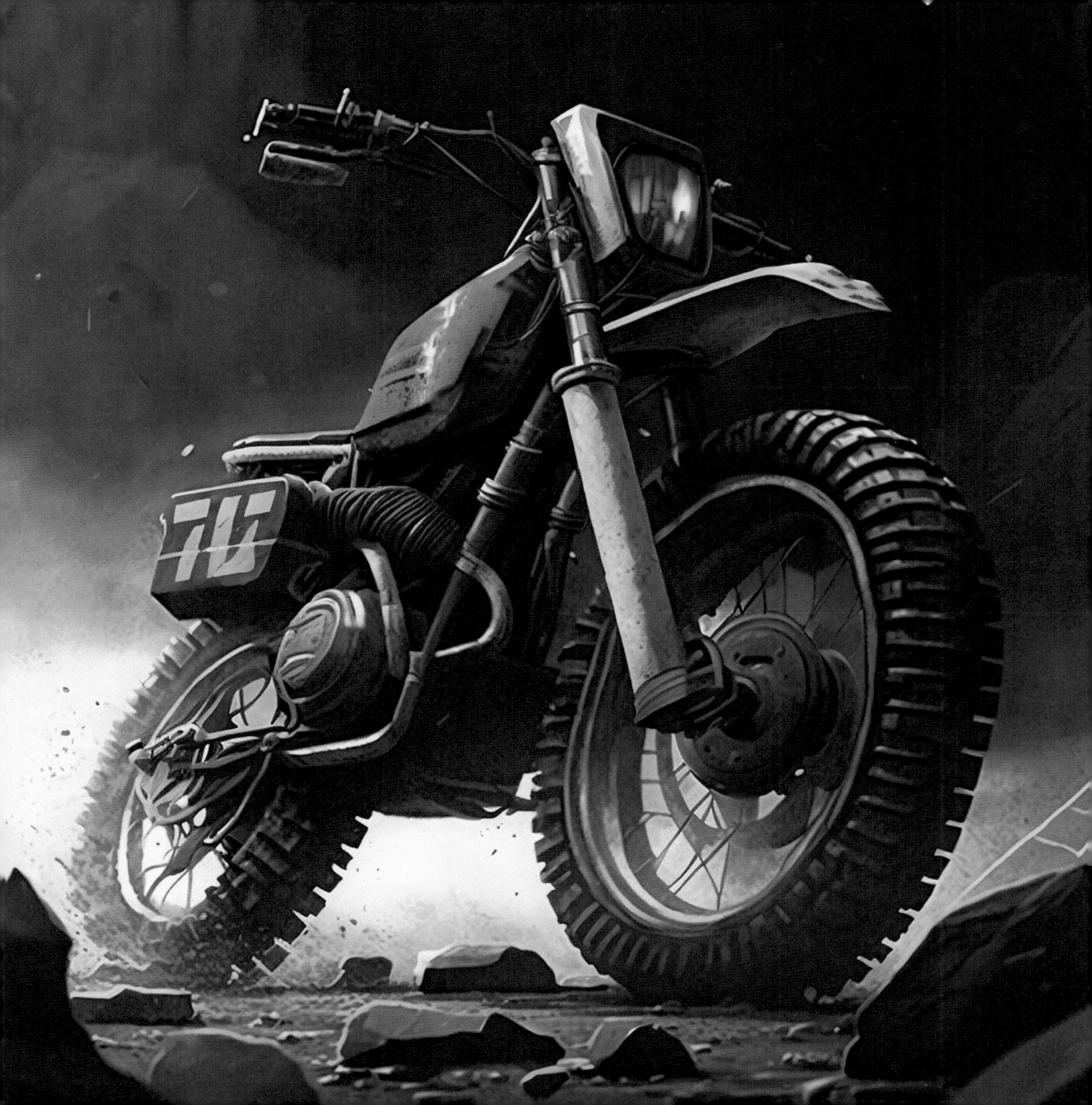

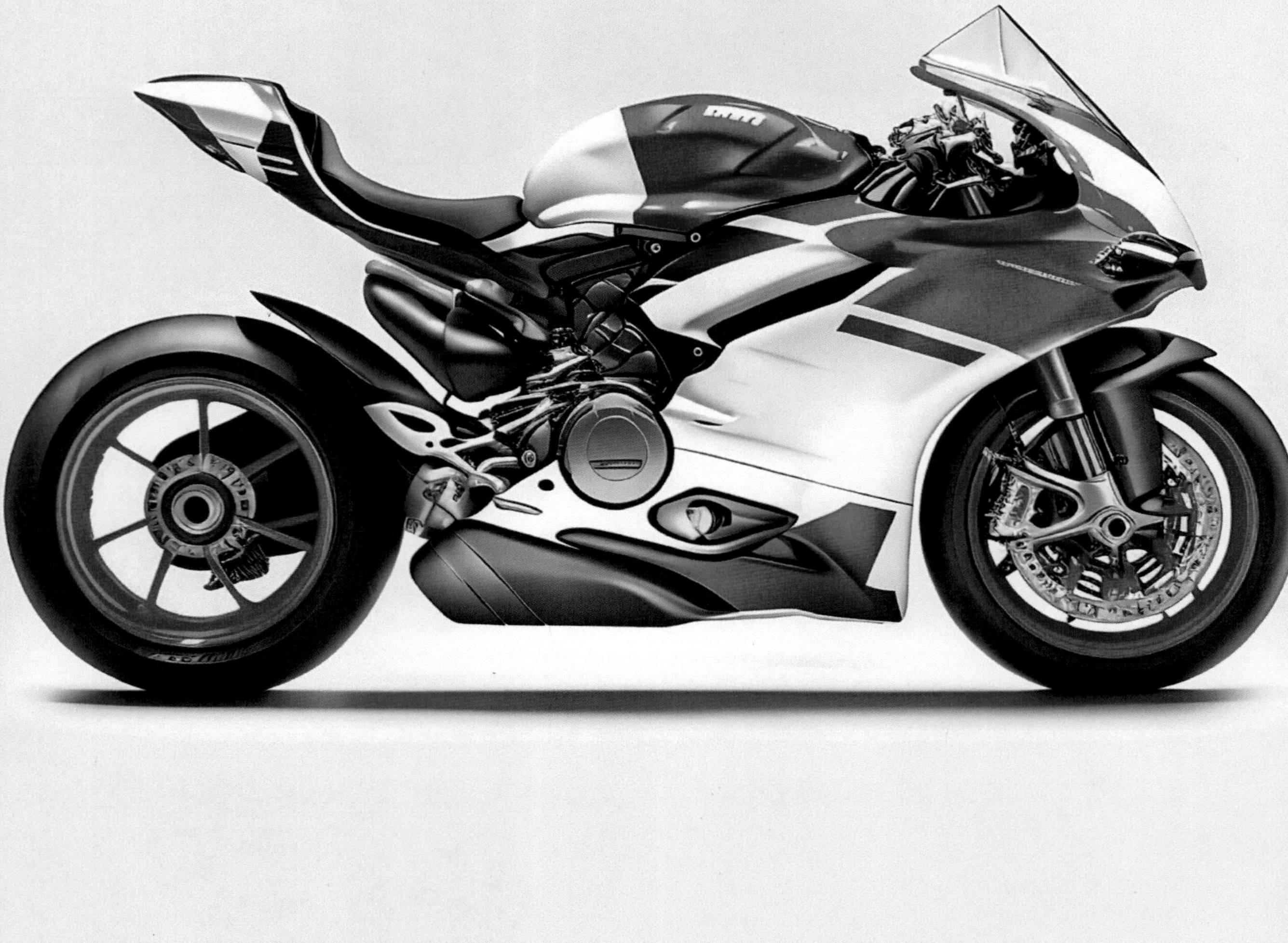

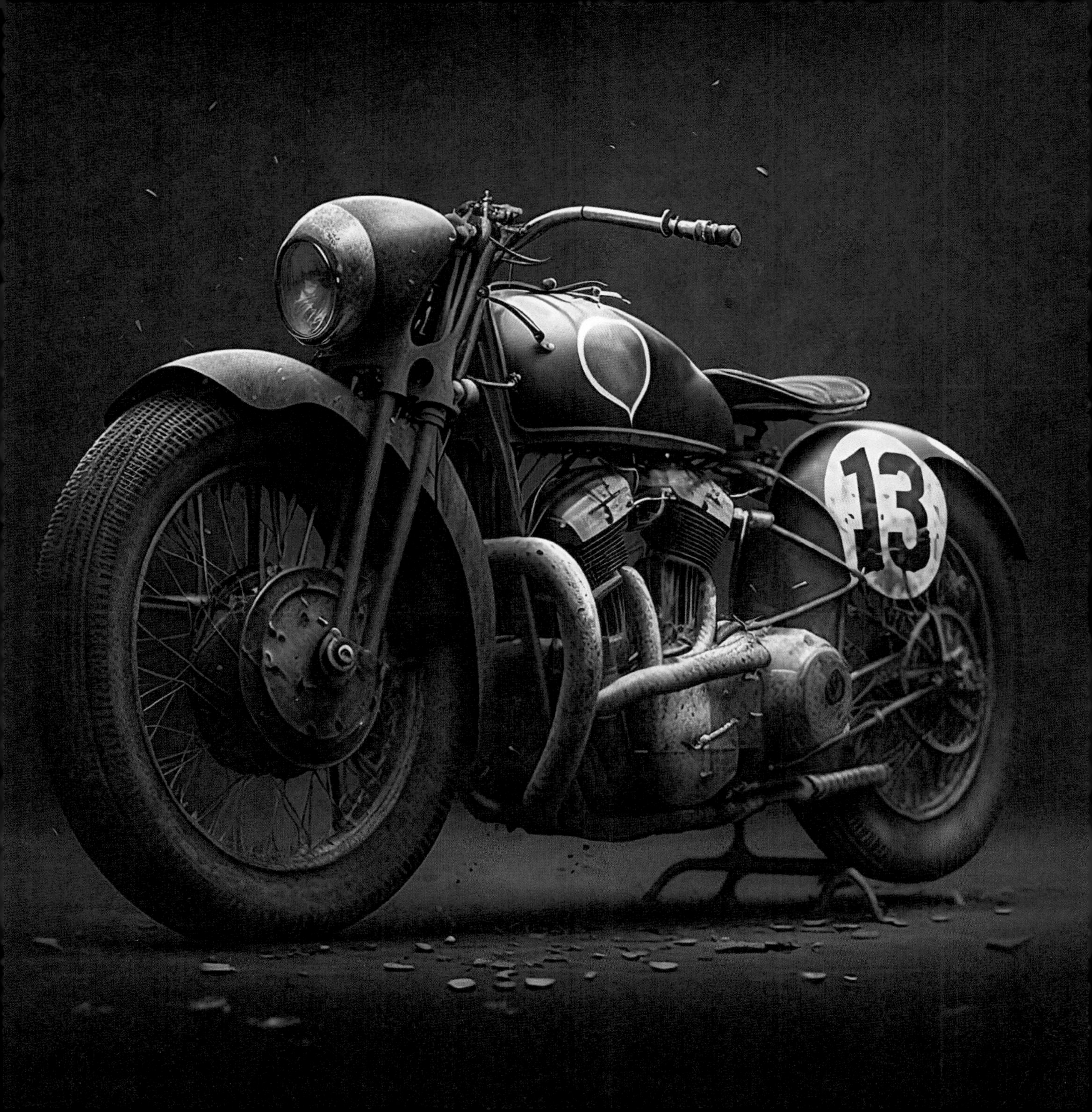
13

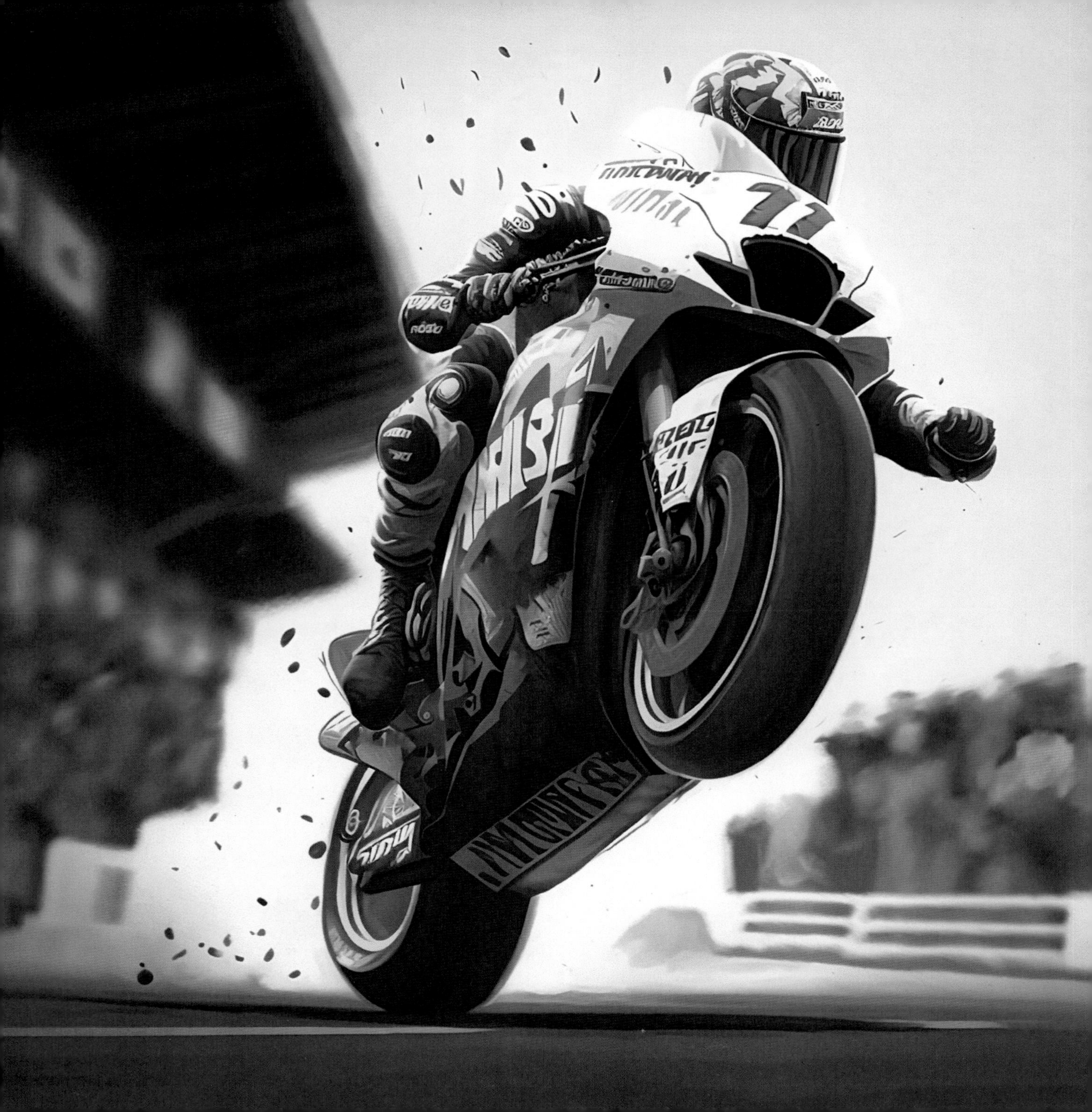

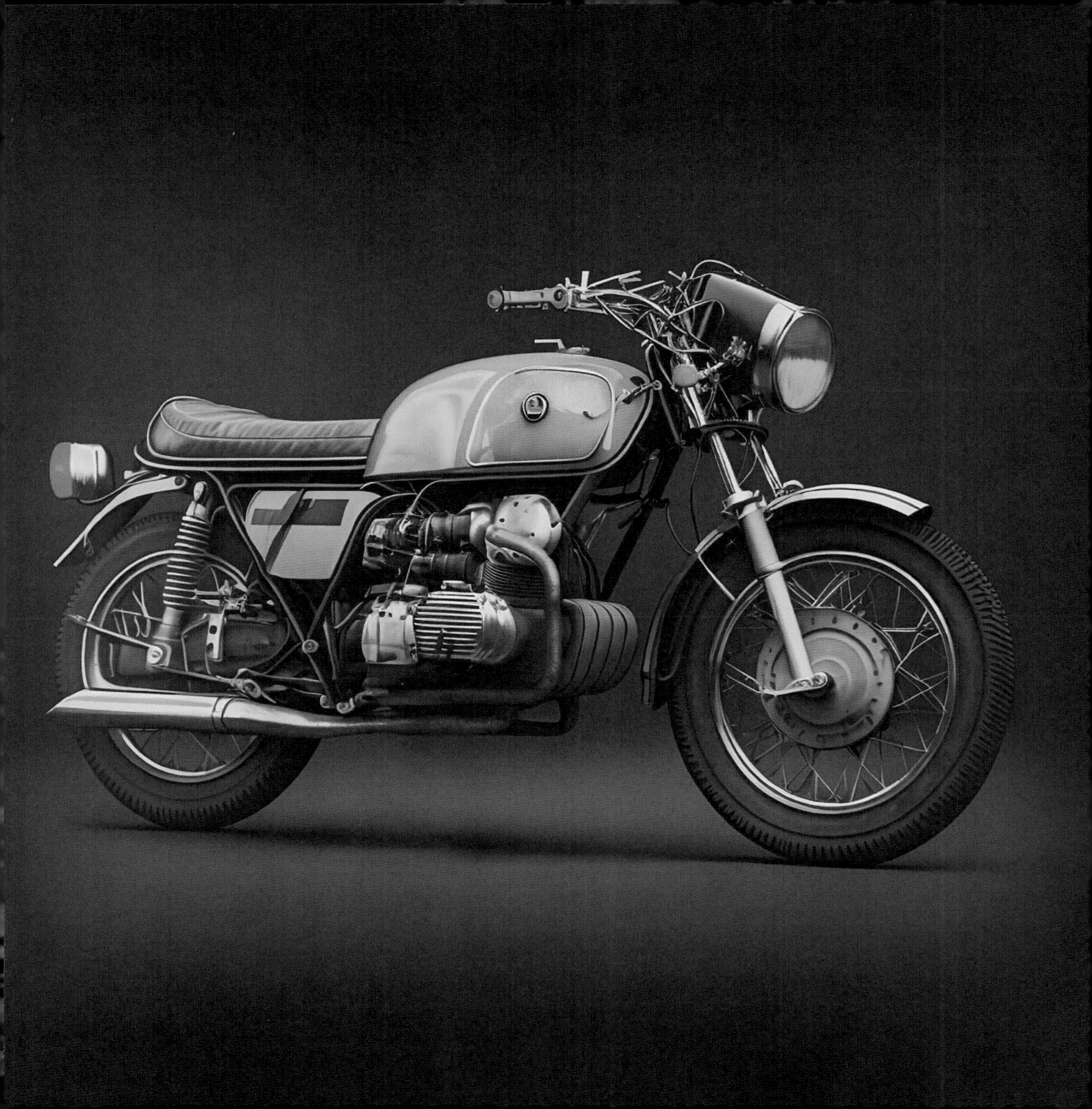

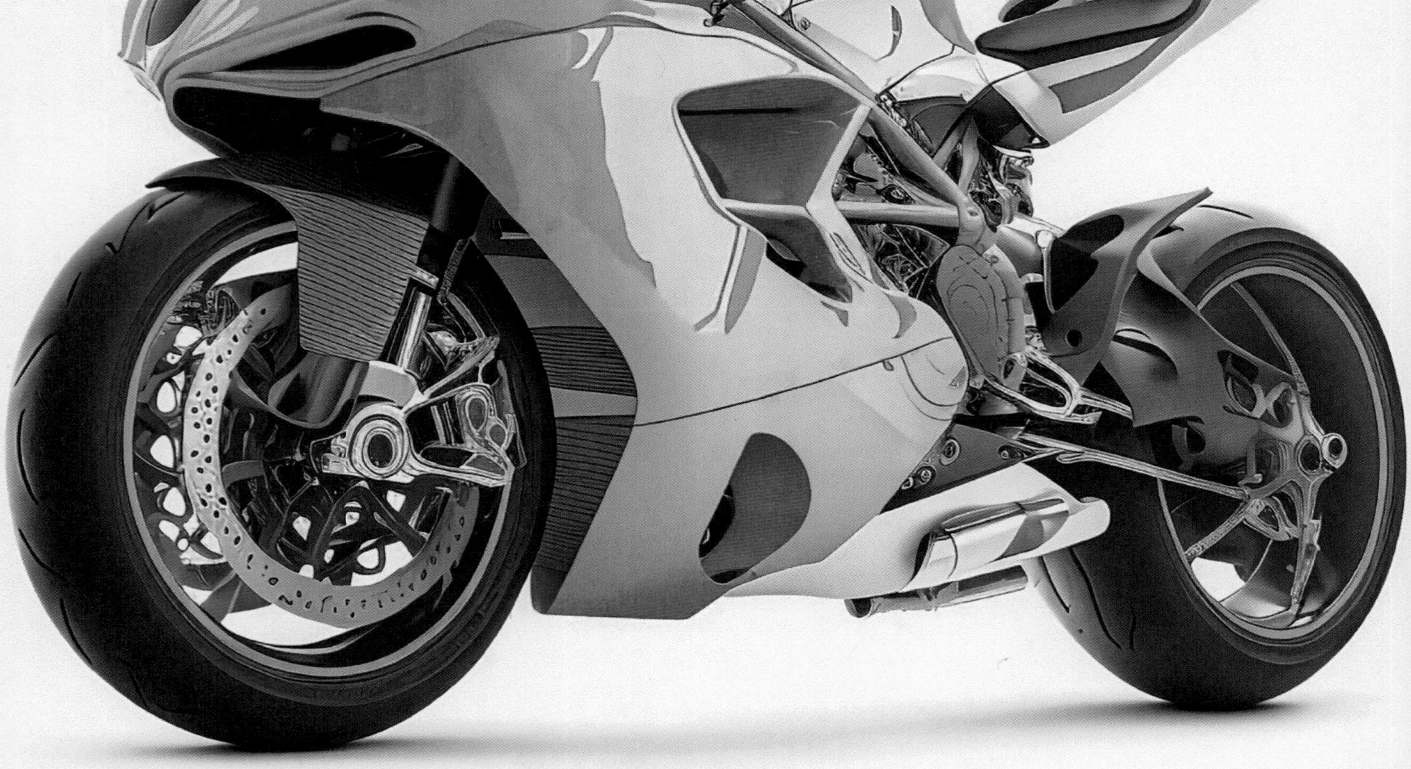

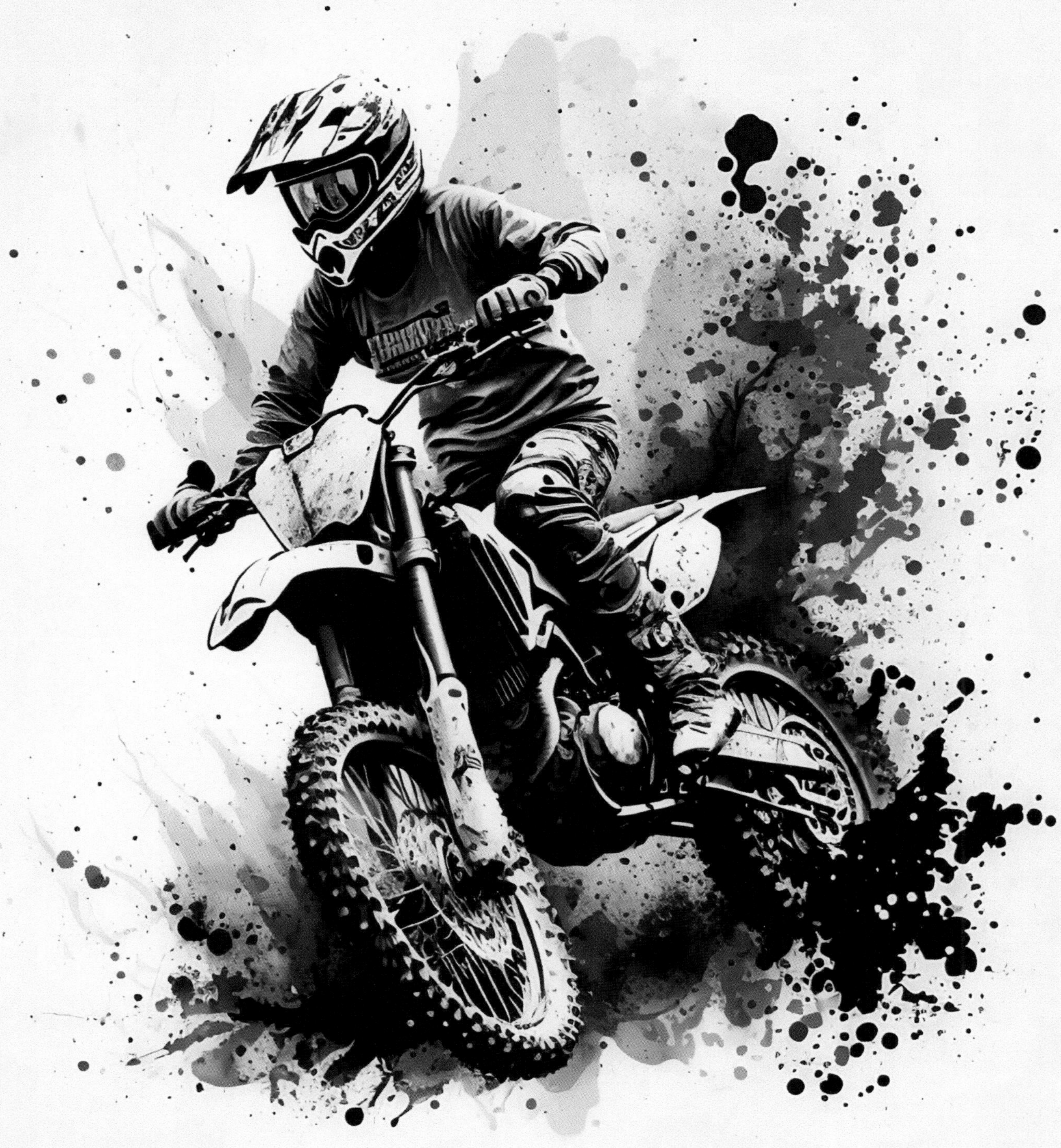

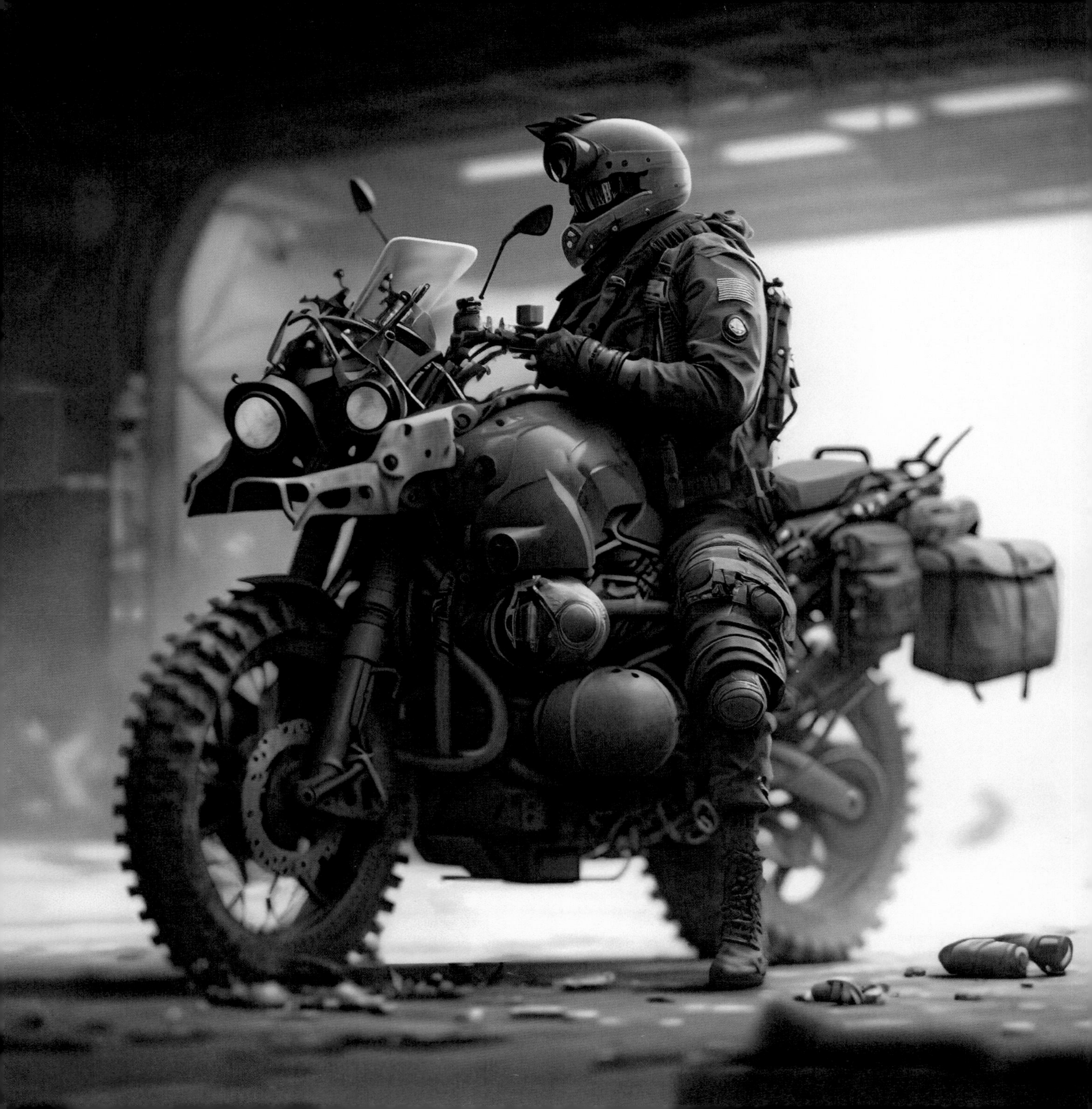

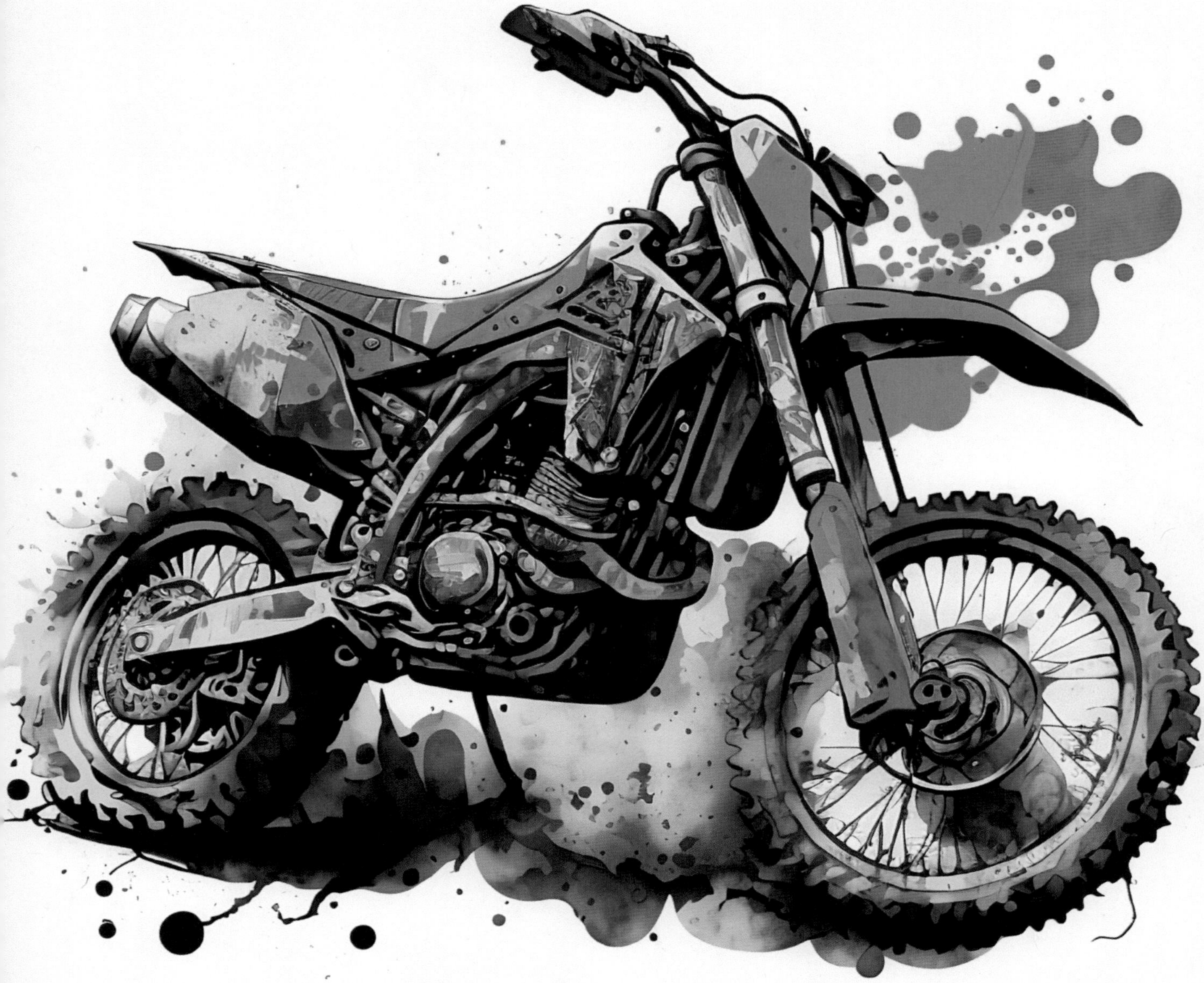

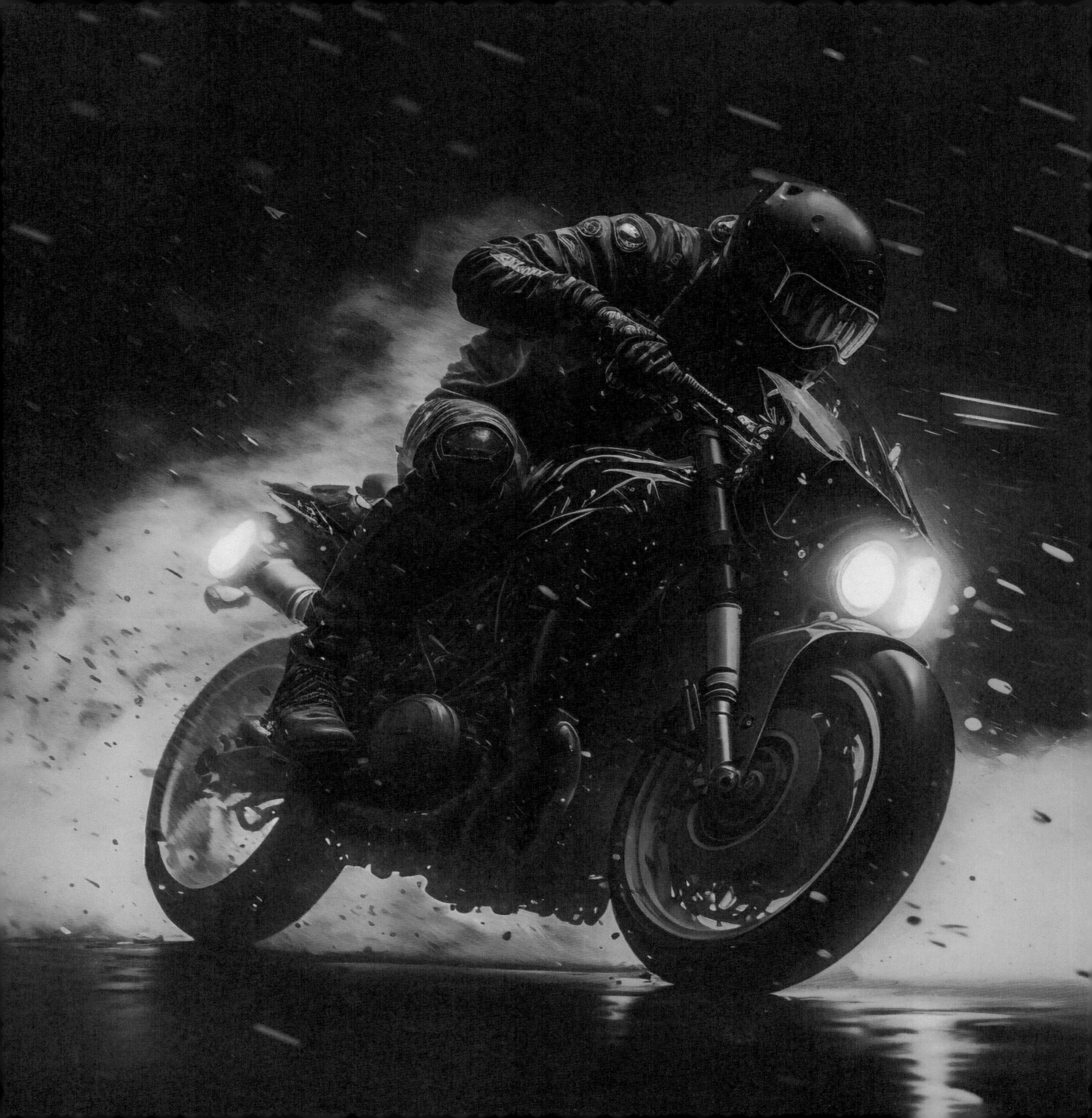

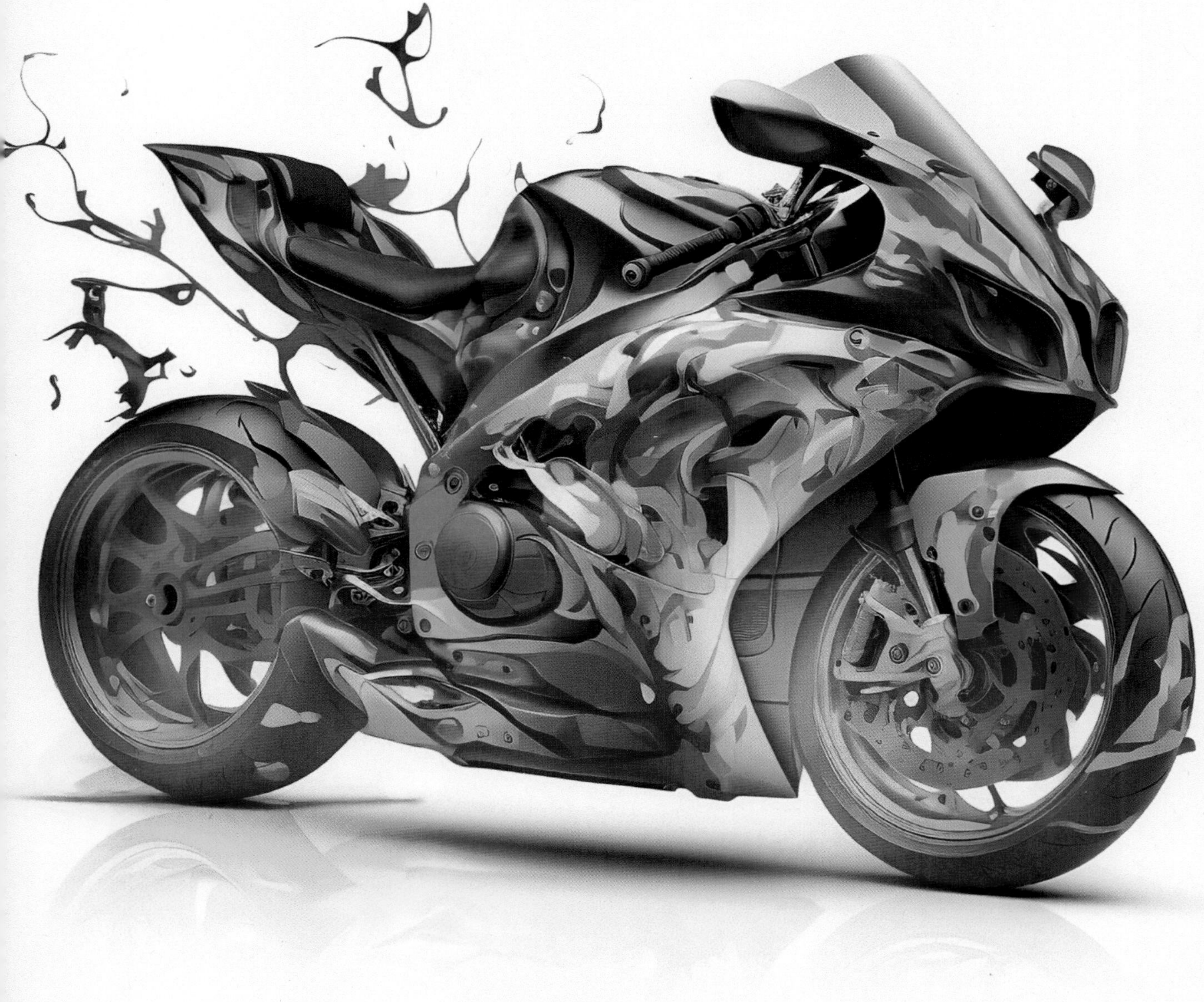

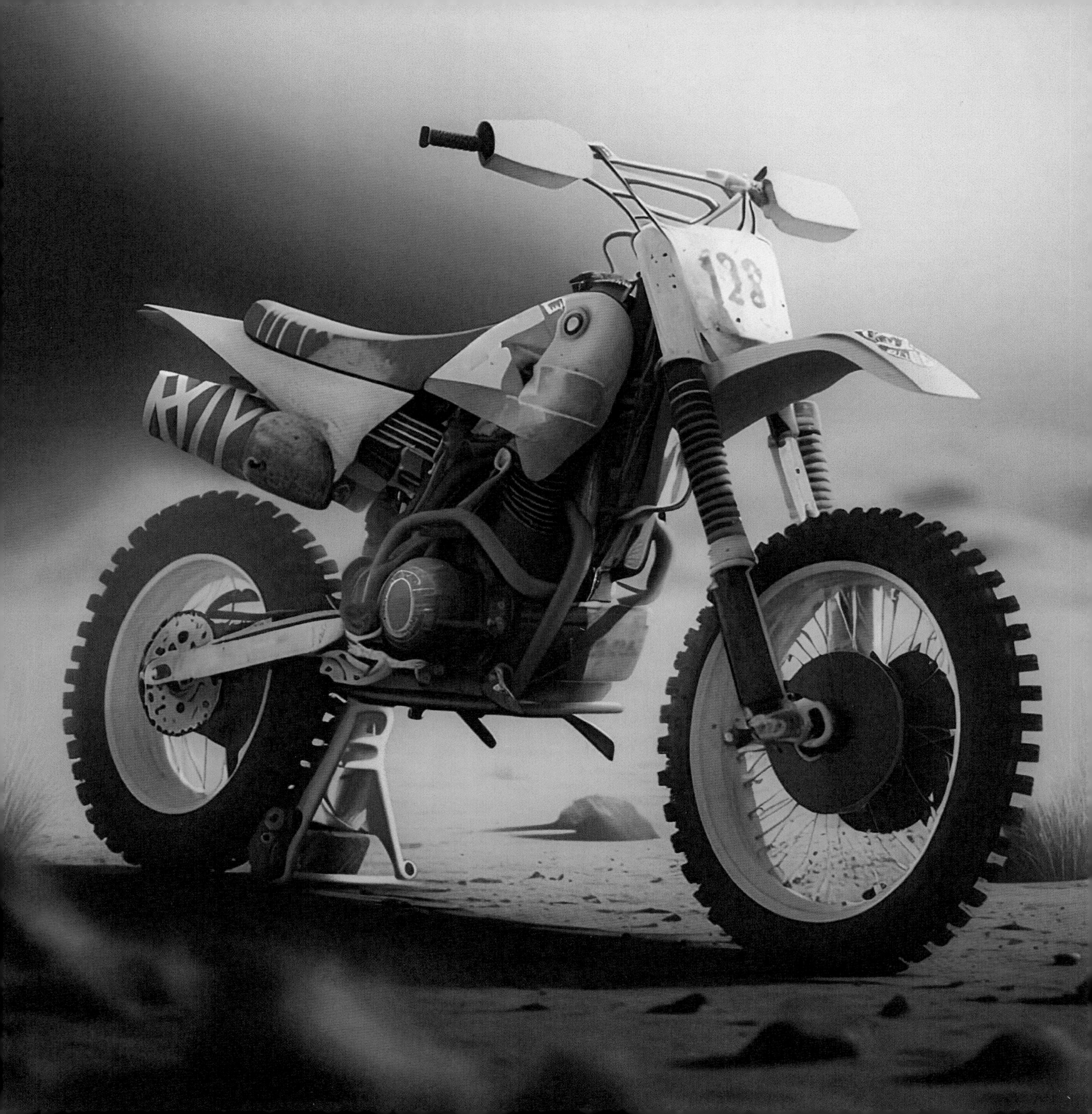
128

Printed by Amazon Italia Logistica S.r.l.
Torrazza Piemonte (TO), Italy

49073201R00020